BEER TERRAIN

FROM FIELD TO GLASS

Jonathan Cook

For information about special discounts for bulk purchases,
please contact Satya House at 413-477-8743 or sales@satyahouse.com

Publisher's Cataloging-In-Publication Data
(*Prepared by The Donohue Group, Inc.*)

Cook, Jonathan, 1970-
    Beer terrain : from field to glass / Jonathan Cook.

    pages : illustrations ; cm

    Issued also as an ebook.
    ISBN: 978-1-935874-30-0

    1. Microbreweries—New England.   2. Microbreweries—New York (State)
3. Farms, Small—New England.   4. Farms, Small—New York (State)   5. Local foods—
New England.   6. Local foods—New York (State)   I. Title.

TP573.U6 C66 2015
338.76634209746   2014955301

ISBN: 978-1-935874-31-7 (e-book)
LCCN: 2014955301

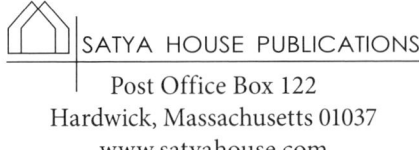

SATYA HOUSE PUBLICATIONS
Post Office Box 122
Hardwick, Massachusetts 01037
www.satyahouse.com

ACKNOWLEDGMENTS

I owe a debt of gratitude to many people, including the folks who took time from pioneering the return of native beer to share their stories with me. Special thanks go out to my one-time publisher at Lakshmi Books, Liz Steele, for offering to publish the story just the way I described it in my proposal. That didn't work out, but I never would have completed this without her encouragement. When I was trying to figure out what to do with the finished manuscript, I turned to friend and colleague from our newspaper days, Cristy Bertini. She gave me confidence and directed me to my current publisher, Satya House. I thank both of them. Also, I need to thank Rich Angers, my friend for almost forty years now, for loaning me his lake house where I was able to get the writing jump-started in seclusion. And of course, I should thank my partner, collaborator, author of Chapter 8, and wife of many years, Suzanne. Thanks for the exbeeriences!

CONTENTS

INTRODUCTION

his book is about the terrain of a very special movement in
craft brewing. It's about beer with *terroir*. Brewing in a way that
reflected the landscape and climate, as well as the craft and skill of the
farmers, maltsters and brewers, was a cultural norm for thousands of
years. Today it is rare, but healthy and growing fast. Locally brewed
beer represents an economic and cultural wave of change in the craft
brew industry that I began exploring right in my own backyard of
New England.

As I studied the maps and travelled the roads that took my
collaborator and me through the achingly beautiful landscape—from
farm to pub, mountains to beaches, season to season—I began to

get a deep sense of the complexity in this terrain. I learned how the variation from one pocket valley to the next rocky hillside contributes to a substantial variety in the grain and hops grown there. This beer is of this land, and just so happens to taste really good.

The reason we have this beer today is because a few intrepid artisans decided to pour themselves into the labor of making it happen. This is a story about the people, the land, and the process that makes for very special beer. It's about the beer terrain.

There's another story here, too. It's about two different versions of capitalism. One is the global supply network that sells grain on the commodities market and homogenizes the malt, distributing it world-wide via vast petroleum-based transit systems. The other involves a handshake and a short drive in a small truck. In the end, the global system produces consistency that is easily branded. The handshake economy yields a unique product with expanding market demand.

Farmers and brewers have learned to thrive by being small and independent. Working together they've created native beers with un-paralleled freshness and character.

Beer from Here

Park Avenue stretches north and south on the west side of Worcester, Massachusetts. From the foot of Dead Horse Hill to Gold Star Boulevard, fast food chains, used car lots, and dive bars line the street. One notable exception is tranquil Elm Park, with arched footbridges and enormous shade trees. Another is Peppercorn's Grille & Tavern, a neighborhood original where my wife, Suzanne, and I make our way into the bar.

A large window along the back wall looks into what used to be an ice cream store and is now Wormtown Brewery. There, perched on a ladder and peering down into the stainless steel mash tun, cofounder Ben Roesch practices his trade the same way hundreds of other brewers throughout New England do every day—a special combination of chemistry and basic plumbing. Heat the mash, boil the wort, pitch the yeast, etc. In between each step, the liquid needs to be moved through piping and hoses to the next stage in the system. Each vessel needs to be cleaned out and sanitized between every use. Rubber boots are required gear.

What sets Roesch apart in the brewing world happens before most brewers enter the picture. It starts when he visits the agricultural fields that grow his grains and hops. Though the cost of land in Massachusetts is the third highest in the nation, small farms still dot the rural communities to the west and north of this centrally located city.

The microbrew revolution made its way to these parts in the mid-1980s and set roots by the early 1990s. Almost from the beginning, many brewers occasionally used local ingredients like honey or fruit. While Roesch has incorporated these adjunct-type ingredients himself over the years, he says, with Wormtown, "We wanted to take it to the next level." Not only do some of the specialty brews contain locally sourced contents, but the year-round offerings all use at least 5 percent Massachusetts-grown ingredients. As it says on the Wormtown pints, "A little Mass in every glass."

This glass in front of me, on the other hand, boasts 100 percent Massachusetts-grown hops and malt. In fact, every ounce is grown within forty miles of the brewery—a ground-breaking achievement in an industry that ironically markets itself as being local. A basic tenet of the successful craft brew business model is to associate the brewery with the locale and describe the product as local and fresh. This incomplete portrait has even slipped through to the local food scene. At "locavore" dinners, the beer is always brewed locally, but often the harvest happens across the continent or on the other side of the Atlantic Ocean.

The reality of the New England beer industry is this: parts are assembled here, creatively and with very tasty results, but the production of the main ingredients usually happens thousands of miles away. Such an arrangement has far-reaching consequences in economics, conservation, and the character of the beer itself, all of which may impact the brewery's bottom line. Yet, the beer in my hand represents a tidal shift in the thriving regional craft beer industry. Many brewers are finding customers receptive to the notion that delicious beer can be made with ingredients provided by local farmers. Many would argue that beer made with local ingredients could offer unique results unobtainable anywhere else.

Affectionately dubbed "MassWhole Hop Session," this dark ruby-hued beverage begins with a hoppy spice aroma and continues through notes of soft bread and black walnut. Surprisingly light in body and only 3.7 percent alcohol, this drink makes for a relaxing session. Full flavor and easy going down, the surrounding terrain imparts what a wine maker would covetously call *terroir*. A French word, terroir loosely means "sense of place." Grapes cultivated on the coast of Buzzards Bay develop characteristics unlike grapes grown in Santa Barbara County. In the glass is the essence of the terrain, a window on a unique region. As such, wine that expresses terroir can distinguish itself in a crowded field.

The businessman in Roesch knows that identifying his product with local culture and landmarks can only endear him to his customers who, after all, are locals themselves. "We sell 90 percent of our beer in central Mass. Our customers live locally," he says, acknowledging, "Without them, we would be nothing."

Wormtown Brewery gets its name from one of the city's many pseudonyms. Roesch's beers follow suit. "Be Hoppy" is a take on the omnipresent yellow Smiley Face, invented here in Worcester. "Turtle Boy Blueberry Ale" honors a unique memorial statue near the city common. Of course, a lot of small brewers play this name game. A modest-sized brewery has to have a local following to survive, but Roesch's pride of place extends well beyond marketing.

A central Massachusetts product himself, Roesch sees Wormtown's "local first" practices as a way to complete the economic cycle in a sustainable way. He notes that when supplies travel fewer miles, they use fewer resources, such as gasoline. Also, patronizing local suppliers keeps the currency in the local economy, which strengthens the market for his product.

"I'm only doing what I'm asking my customers to do," he says. Plus, he feels a kinship with area farmers. "For us, there are a lot of similarities. We're both small businesses."

Before Roesch became a business owner, he got soil under his nails as an employee of an organic farm. Having studied forestry and conservation at the University of Massachusetts, he was hired to tap the maples and cut firewood at Land's Sake, a community owned farm in the town of Weston. In the summer, he worked the fields. Among the crops he helped cultivate were pumpkins which, naturally, he brought with him to his first brewery job at Cambridge Brewing Company—a telling start to his career.

Later, he got closer to what he's doing now with a spell as the head brewer and distiller for Nashoba Valley Winery, where he worked orchard fruits and other local ingredients into his seasonal brews, all the while rubbing elbows with the winemaking world where the encompassing terrain provides entirely for the bottle's contents.

And now, we have Wormtown: evocative of a place literally in the land, where soil nourishes the crops and the profile of the beer begins to formulate. Not surprisingly, grain cultivated by small farmers in the northeast climate differs from that of the Great Plains.

"This stuff definitely gives its own flavor," Roesch says. Malted in small batches and often harvested from a single farm, the local supply provides a variety of flavors. "For brewers," Roesch says, "this is both a blessing and a challenge."

He points out that consistency is one of the common tenets of successful brewing, at least among the flagship, year-round flavors. Major malt companies tend to use products of monoculture, harvested by massive combines and blended to supply the demand for a product that tastes the same every time. What's more, he says, local malt costs two to three times the price of the well-travelled stuff. Instead of ordering online, he says, "I have to go out there working to secure supplies, which takes time away from my real job, which is brewing beer."

Challenging, yes, but that's what separates the artisan from the beer factory worker. Creativity has been the hallmark of the craft beer world, as the trend toward seasonal and one-of-a-kind brews demonstrates. This is the realm where local suppliers have made strong inroads. While most beer is made with hops grown on boundless acres in the northwestern United States or Europe, then dried and formed into pellets, New England hop growers are exclusively small farms, typically limiting production to one or two acres of land.

One technique that would be impractical without a nearby harvest is "wet hopping," which calls for hops to be picked and tossed into the kettle on the same day. Roesch explains that wet hopping provides more floral aromatic properties with a less aggressive bittering component than dried hops. Local malt is also fresher, Roesch says, going from malt house to mash tun within a day or two.

Conversely, the giants of the malting world store the blended harvests in silos until demand catches up with supply, creating months of idle time with each day leeching volatile flavor compounds bit by bit.

Whether it's local identity, vibrant ingredients, or just plain great tasting beer, something is working for Wormtown. After they celebrated their second anniversary in spring 2012 by tapping kegs of a Double India Pale Ale made with local rye and buckwheat, the brewery began searching for bigger digs. Their space in Peppercorn's Grille & Tavern was so cramped, they had to remove the drop ceiling to open the mash tun.

Around the brewery's third birthday—celebrated by the release of a Double Rye IPA made with Massachusetts grown crystal malt— Roesch and company moved their operations to Shrewsbury Street, also known as Worcester's "restaurant row." There, they can brew three to six times its former capacity. Six thousand barrels of beer or 186,000 gallons will be made there in the coming year. That translates into a lot more acreage made profitable for local farmers and a solid market foothold for native beer.

In the meantime, he says, "We'll still have 5 percent Massachusetts malt and 5 percent hops." In fact, he adds, "This year we hope to increase it." As far as the rotating line of MassWholes, Roesch has begun to keep one in stock at all times. Is it the taste of their home state that has people buying Wormtown?

"I think what's really drawing interest is the everyday guy," he says. "He realizes it's local and that might get him to try it, but it's also approachable."

In other words, Wormtown manages to craft highly drinkable beers while introducing locally produced malt and hops. Roesch puts it simply, "People are diggin' the beer."

Being at the forefront of this surging growth, Roesch was tapped to sit on the advisory committee for the Massachusetts Local Ingredients in Brewing Project, a Massachusetts Department of Agriculture initiative staffed by Bonita Oehlke. Using federal grant money to conduct a survey of local brewers, Oehlke says the idea is to calculate the value of local ingredients currently in use and match that number with the total cost of ingredients used in the state. "Growers need to be exposed to this exciting opportunity in terms of new customers."

A second grant will finance the development of a locavore beer trail, complete with a map of brewers and growers. Other regions have adopted such marketing tools, but unlike most beer trails, businesses in this case are highlighted for their support of the farming community.

SWEET TATS

Of course, if the beer didn't knock people's socks off, it wouldn't matter where the ingredients came from. No one knows this better than Jackie Cawley. Suzanne and I met Cawley when we stopped in at a new restaurant on Water Street and struck up a conversation with her over a pint of Wormtown's Seven Hills Pale Ale. Turned out not only was Cawley our bartender, but she also worked a day job as a sales rep for Wormtown. Presto! A piece of the story fell into my lap. Immediately, I knew that Cawley's perspective was vital to answering an important question: Are the locally grown ingredients in Wormtown's beer important to the customers?

Cawley, who focuses on bars and restaurants, starts her pitch by offering a taste of the product. "A lot of people are shocked," she says. "They can't believe a little local brewer made beer taste this good."

They have to like the beer because it's too new to come with a reputation. But once that is established, Cawley talks up the local aspects of the brewery—the locale as well as the local ingredients, and invariably, businesses like that, too.

"They want to carry something local on tap," she says. "It's the way the world is going. Support local, support local." Do it often enough and business owners start to see how closely they depend on each other.

For example, one account Cawley opened, Tomasso Trattoria in Southborough, learned that Wormtown gives its spent grain to a farmer for use as livestock feed. Turns out, Tomasso purchases its pork from the same farm. Now they serve the beer to go with it. The cycle never leaves the area. A local farmer grows grain. A local maltster malts the grain. A local brewer makes the beer. A local farmer feeds his pig. And a local restaurant serves the pork paired with the beer that tied them all together.

"It's like a cycle of life thing," says Cawley. "Pretty cool."

Not only has Cawley helped Wormtown expand their tap accounts, but she has helped them to expand their offerings as well. As a self-proclaimed lover of breakfast stout, Cawley suggested Roesch add one to the Wormtown line-up. To decide on a recipe, she brought him her two favorites: Founder's Breakfast Stout and Montreal brewer Dieu du Ciels Aphrodite, and asked him to make something that combined characteristics. With oatmeal and vanilla beans creating a deeply smooth flavor, the cocoa nibs and locally roasted coffee brings a sunny complexion to its character. The beer needed only a name.

Roesch found inspiration in his sales rep's tattoo. Vivid with flowers and colorful insects, Cawley's arm is always a summer day. "I got it for my kids," she says. "My son loves bugs and I love flowers." A piece from the tattoo—a bumble bee on a sunflower—became the label art and the brew was dubbed "Sweet Tats."

True to the local economy at every turn, when Wormtown held a release party for the new beer, they welcomed all the area tattoo artists to show off their portfolios.

THE WORMTOWN CONNECTION

A driver in Worcester will often encounter dozens of memorial "squares" on a jaunt across the city. Really just intersections with plaques, hundreds of these places dot the map, but probably the most famous, or infamous to some, is Kelley Square, where no less than seven city streets converge.

Littered by an assortment of traffic signs and broken headlight glass, anyone who ever takes the wrong exit off interstate 290 will surely recall the feeling of wanting to stop in the middle of the intersection and scream, "Who the hell has the right of way?!" But it works on old-fashioned common sense and an opportunistic attitude. The timid often sit, counting cars going by until prompted forward by the blaring of horns.

One corner business has been around even longer than the World War I Memorial at Kelley Square. The Hotel Vernon, which has gained popularity among the young party crowd for the live music and dollar drafts, has remained largely unchanged over the years.

At a time when many of the old, dark drinking joints, like the Boynton, have remodeled to capture the craft beer crowd, the Vernon feels like an antique. In the basement are remnants of a 1920s speakeasy called the Madame Rhubarb. Back in the day, patrons would refer to the undercover bar as "The Yacht Club." With thirty-four rooms, the Vernon is technically a hotel, but I don't know of anyone who has ever stayed there except Babe Ruth, who reportedly spent one winter, early in his career, lingering in the hospitable confines. He is said to have come back season after season, apparently afflicted with a condition I have also endured: chronic Worcester craving.

Since I first pushed through the saloon door of the Vernon many years ago and felt the eyes of the barflies upon me, I have come to expect yellow factory-made beer, always in a mug. I end up having a little whisky to wash out the aftertaste and help cut the foam or I might just skip the dollar bargain altogether. The only other choices were all the same rice and corn beers just wearing different labels. Always, I wished they had one tap for a craft beer. Until 2010, this historic institution resisted all taste trends.

It's easy to see why. In the barroom, the walls are covered in century-old murals depicting Coleridge's *Rime of the Ancient Mariner*. Painted by local artists, a few of whom went on to some acclaim, the intricate work is coated in the grit of time and tobacco smoke, making it difficult to appreciate in the dim light. The tale depicts a sailor who killed an albatross and forever after was cursed.

How Wormtown integrated the Vernon's tap lines is a happier story. The Vernon, owned by Bob Largess, was on Wormtown's list of potential accounts back when Roesch was the only salesman. "In Worcester we have our share of places with character," he says, "and the Vernon is certainly one of them." But he couldn't just drop in for an impromptu meeting. "If you wanted to see Captain Bob (as folks call Largess) you could only do it between 9 and 11 on Wednesday mornings. He sits at a round table. All the sales reps sit at the bar. They know what order they came in."

With such an arrangement, everyone is privy to all the discussions. When it came Roesch's turn, Largess put him on the spot, asking what he thought of Pabst Blue Ribbon. Not wanting to offend any of the other sales reps, Roesch deftly sidestepped and answered, "I want to help you sell more beer. Whatever is your slow-selling beer, we'll replace that." Captain Bob responded with "I'll give you a call." To Roesch, that didn't sound promising. "I figured that was it. A couple months later he stopped by the brewery and said 'I've tasted it. You've got staying power. Send over a couple of kegs.'"

While The Vernon has made its home in the city for over a hundred years, it has stronger agricultural connections than one might think. For one thing, Largess owns a significant amount of farmland. He also gives tours of the Kelley Square neighborhood in a stagecoach pulled by his own Clydesdales. Furthermore, the beer on tap, once again, starts with area farms, just as it must have in the Vernon's 19th century beginnings.

On a cold and windy night, Suzanne and I stop in hoping for live music in the back. Called the Ship Room, swinging doors open onto what looks like the cabin of a fine sailing vessel. Tonight it's closed up, so we settle into a game of pool. This is a great place to play pool if you enjoy challenges. While the table surface itself seems level, the floor takes a drastic dip at one end so it feels like standing on the slope of a swimming pool. Even so, we are having too much fun for mere mortals. It helps that the Wormtown Brewery banner graces the short row of tap handles. Not surprisingly, from the entire spectrum of flavors Wormtown makes, here they pour a pale, straw-colored, easy drinking Kölsch. In fact, the only hard part is stopping at two, since they are served in frosty mugs and slide down the hatch as effortlessly as any liquid known to man.

Somehow, we manage to break away and drive towards home with one more destination in mind. Back in our hometown, but not wanting the night to end, we stop by the Hexmark Tavern of the Salem Cross Inn. Here we continue the Wormtown evening with a Seven Hills Pale Ale by the fireplace. The thought that I cannot escape is that drinking Wormtown not only gives me a warm glow, but strengthens the community in which I live. Some may argue with that, but every glass of Wormtown represents the fruit of local farming and at least five profitable economic transactions, all involving locally and independently owned businesses. That's simply not the same positive impact found in most other beers. When most products are purchased, the money flies all over the world, fleeing the community and enriching a distant corporation, often at the cost of the environment and local farmland. As I drain my glass, I am convinced of my good deed.

FLAVORS OF THE BAY STATE

Wormtown's native beer lineup begins with the MassWhole series. Each MassWhole contains 100 percent Massachusetts-sourced malt and hops. As I write, a Hefeweizen is on a six-month run. This one is brewed with wheat and magnum hops from Four Star Farms in Northfield, as well as barley grown in Hadley at Czajkowski Farm. Described as Bavarian style, this unfiltered, hazy brew hints of cloves, which is primarily the result of the style's traditional yeast. Several other MassWhole flavors, including the Hop Session and Amber have been brewed as well, but are now out of stock. No worries, Roesch is planning on a rotational, often one-of-a-kind offering with MassWhole.

Local First was an early predecessor to MassWhole. This Bitter was made with 100 percent organic barley grown at Carter's Farm in Plainfield, Massachusetts. Going back even further was the Misty Brook Wet Hop Harvest Double Pale Ale. Roesch looked at this one as a celebration of the harvest. Made with unmalted wheat and rye from

Misty Brook Farm in Hardwick and Maine-grown malted barley, the topper was the fresh picked Willamette hops, which Roesch had shipped overnight from the northwest. That happened only a few short years ago.

Things have changed quite a bit since then, as Roesch sees for himself when he visits the area's up and coming hop farms. Fresh hops are now no more than an hour round trip from his doorstep.

Even so, the most important development to Wormtown's mission has to be the malt house down the road. After all, without malt, there is no beer. "Before them," Roesch says, "this just wasn't possible. Valley Malt is taking the bull by the horns."

LOCAVORE PIONEERS

On a broad neck of land formed by a bend in the Connecticut River, the Hadley, Massachusetts town common stretches for about a mile from north to south. Behind all the homes bordering the common extends the telltale patchwork of cropland. This is the heart of the Pioneer Valley—one of the first breadbaskets in the North American colonies. It is said that in the mid-1600s, every farmer who settled along the banks of the river cultivated wheat.

Only a quarter-mile from the common, Suzanne and I arrive at what appears to be a two-car garage. The pleasing aroma of warm bread welcomes us to this unique place on the New England craft beer scene—Valley Malt.

About one hundred sacks of finished product sit in rows, ready for delivery. Behind them is Andrea Stanley, slight of frame but large in stature. We found her working in a sweatshirt, jeans, and rubber boots. The mask she wears helps her breathe easier in the haze of grain dust that hangs in the air and touches down on every surface. Like a carpenter coated in sawdust or a potter freckled with clay, we see before us an artisan plying her craft.

Andrea and her husband, Christian, own New England's only malt house. After receiving a strong handshake, I ask where the batch in front of us came from. She says the barley, a two-row pale ale variety, grew at Lakeview Farm in New York. Within the day, it will be delivered to a brewery in another part of the Northeast, where it will be turned into beer and enjoyed by people living in the same region.

That cycle of supply meeting demand in the New England and New York region has not been active since before Prohibition. Since late 2010, when the Stanley's opened their little business, farmers are finding a new market for grain and brewers have begun to cultivate beer of the native terrain.

As wineries have always known, there is something to be said for where the fruit grows. Temperatures, seasons, winds, water, and numerous other factors play into the character of the grape, or in the case of beer, the grain. The qualities imparted by each region's climate infuse the final product with a complexion that can't be replicated elsewhere.

Prior to Valley Malt, brewers from this area did not have a local option among malt suppliers. Maine potato farmers have been rotating malting barley in their fields and selling the harvest to industry giant, Canada Malt. At first, these grains were blended in with everything else, but at about the same time Valley Malt came on line, Canada Malt began marketing the Maine-grown barley as its own regional brand. Prior to that, the "place" tasted in the product of northeastern brewers came out of central Europe or the American northwest.

After discovering that fact, Andrea Stanley set out on her present course. From the time she first thought about starting a malt house, she immersed herself in learning and perfecting the craft. Recently she was able to leave a job as a caseworker and dedicate all of her professional energy to the production of malt with terroir.

Now in her fifth year, she sinks herself into her daily work with the devotion of one who has found a calling. As she explained it to me, the challenge of creating something new, that also makes sense for the environment and strengthens the local economy, makes for a satisfying day's labor. Standing before us, literally covered in her work, Andrea is generous with her time. I load our purchase, a ten-pound sack of pale ale barley malt into the trunk, eager to create our own beer from here.

Having begun a commitment to local food almost fifteen years ago, Suzanne and I have worked for and purchased shares of Community Sponsored Agriculture (CSA) from several small farms across the region. We have also been devoted gardeners with a preference for brewing herbs such as sage, lavender, coriander, and of course, hops. With locally grown malt in hand, we could finally close the loop and make beer that matches our locavore predilections.

Late one evening, a few weeks after our first visit, I have Andrea on the phone. For more than an hour I pose questions while she stands outside on her patio roasting barley and pleasantly explaining the details of her business.

Valley Malt provides for the freshest malt possible and fetches a premium price because of it. Brewers pay sometimes triple for local malt compared to what they pay for the standard global supply. Andrea explains that once the grain is malted, the clock starts ticking. Warehoused malt, like coffee, will lose the desirable aromas that dissipate into the atmosphere and break down over time. This creates a noticeable difference in the nose.

"If wheat or rye sits around, I can tell the difference," Andrea says. "Fresh malt results in a lively beer with full flavors."

Many of the characteristics found in a bottle of beer stem from the malting technique. "A lot of aromas are created in the kiln," she explains. What the brewer gets from the malt house is a sweet, nutty, toasty product that is the backbone of beer.

Again, like coffee, that flavor profile can range from light brown to extremely dark, depending on the method used to produce it. "You can get beans from the same farm and make two totally different coffees," Andrea says. "Part of it has to do with your equipment and part is process, and sort of the technique of the person who's doing it."

Valley Malt makes hand-crafted malts in small, 2,000-pound batches sourced to a single, local and usually organic farm. At the big malt houses, she points out, "It's just more of a process. They blend the malt for a uniform product and pump it out in batches of 30,000 pounds or more."

All malt houses—big or small—follow the same fundamentals. "It's all about time, temperature, and moisture," she says. "If you were to take barley in a big system and just based on time, temperature, and moisture, you could get a pilsner, which is very lightly kilned, gives you lighter color and it also gives you sort of what you expect in a lager. That type of taste. If you go a little bit higher, say, 60 degrees higher at the end of kilning, then you're going to get a lighter pale like an American pale. And if you go a few degrees higher than that, you're going to get English pale. And if you wanted to get around 215 degrees (Fahrenheit) you end up with Munich. That's the highest you can get in the malt vessel."

Following the harvest of plump grains packed with the sweet potential of starch, the seeds are stored for a few weeks. Andrea explains that the dormant period after harvest allows the crop to mature, resulting in maximum germination rates and a quality final product.

After this raw material is done resting, it's brought to the malt house for a warm bath. Valley Malt steeps the grain three times to spur the germination process. This puts enzymes in motion to convert the starch into fermentable sugar, without which there would be no alcohol.

Aside from changing the water, the maltster has another chore during this soak cycle. "When the grain is germinating you have to get in there once a day and you have to stir it," Andrea explains as she leans into the vessel with shovel in hand.

After germination gets underway, the wet seeds are kiln-dried to the brewer's specifications, depending on the desired style of beer. For a darker flavor like chocolate malt or brown malt, the grain will leave the kiln and head to the roaster.

"We have a small drum roaster," Andrea says. "It's a lot like a coffee roaster." It takes seven to nine days for Valley Malt to produce a batch of malt this way.

When it's done, it's fed through a rudimentary machine called a debearder, which removes the stems from the malted grain. The stem, if not dried, would have continued to sprout into a plant. These protein rich stems are then used by farmers who feed the by-product to their cows.

Even as the agricultural resources are supported by Valley Malt's business practices, so are the local energy resources. Since my first visit, a long row of solar panels has been installed in the field behind the malt house. When I walk out there with Andrea in early winter, the panels are surrounded by a quilt of crunchy winter greens and barley seedlings coming up in alternating rows. These power generators stretch out at length and provide all the electricity needs of the business. Another way Valley Malt cuts back on energy imports is with their new heat exchanger that saves 30 percent of energy used during kilning.

Before Valley Malt, virtually all beer made in the Northeast used grain from places like North Dakota, where the combines harvest 1,800 pounds a minute and the monoculture goes on further than the eye can see. In this world of corporate-owned, petroleum-based agriculture, the Stanley's decided to invest their time, money, and talents to establish a foothold, a cottage industry owned by skilled locals, supplied from local sources, and serving local customers. By doing so, they have moved an entire industry closer to sustainability while strengthening the economic fabric in their own backyard.

INDUSTRY REBORN

Not that Andrea could have foreseen her role as a locavore pioneer a few years ago, yet all the Stanleys wanted was to enjoy beer made with locally grown ingredients. A simple thirst for something as fresh as the food they liked to eat led to the discovery that this region's craft breweries, while operated and usually owned locally, have been using malt and hops produced in distant lands.

"We stumbled into it, not having made that connection," Andrea says. "I don't think the word maltster ever entered my ear before, which is kind of crazy considering how much I enjoy beer."

While grain farming in this region has never completely vanished, prior to Valley Malt, brewers had little choice but to rely on major corporate malt producers for their supply. This was not always the case. Before Prohibition, farmers grew grain for beer and malt houses conducted business all across the region.

According to Andrea, the North American malt industry of the twenty-first century has been consolidated into only two large companies. This consolidation, together with Prohibition, long ago snuffed out the local markets. Without a regional malt house to prepare the locally harvested grain, brewers had to acquire malt that traveled thousands of miles before finding its way into "local" craft beer.

Faced with the prospect of having to sacrifice their buy local principles in order to enjoy their beer, the Stanley's took matters into their own hands the way any pioneering spirit would. They planted barley seed in their garden and malted it in their kitchen—and an industry was reborn. Soon the Stanley's had a business plan and a location a few blocks from their home. Christian, a mechanical engineer, designed and built the original system. They contracted with half a dozen farmers to grow brewing grain, and after the summer 2010 harvest, Valley Malt was in business.

Now, they count more than twenty breweries as steady customers and are producing four tons of malt per week, an annual production rate of 400,000 or enough for more than a million pints. Andrea says that though there is enough demand to make more malt, it takes time for the grain supply to catch up.

"We're right in the midst of growing our business," Andrea says. "Last year we were at one ton . . . per week." She points out that the demand side of the equation was evident early on. All she had to do was look at how small farms are bucking a stagnant economy thanks to the vibrant market for farm fresh products. "We're malting twenty-four-seven, three-sixty-five," she says. "It never ends."

All over the Northeast, farmers' markets are popping up on town commons, in mall parking lots, and on city squares. The public wants local food, and no drink is more of a meal than the liquid bread in a pint of beer.

After leaving Hadley, we scoot across the Connecticut River into Northampton for a pint and a few more supplies. We'd be fools not to. In Provisions, a store worth the trip by itself, I had to admire the rows of wine bottles and the display cases of local cheeses and sausages. This is pick-up day for members of a seafood club buying sustainable New England fisheries products. But what has me licking my lips is the beer selection. A man next to me makes a strange grunting noise that seems like a mix of awe and happiness. I can relate. This is primal. Having only two hands, I select two beers made with Valley Malt, a six-pack of Brewmaster Jack's Stray Dog Lager as well as a pair of Jack's Abby concoctions for later.

At home, as I write, I have a glass of Stray Dog in front of me. Caramel color, with off-white foam, malt is forefront here, lacing the mouth with a medium to heavy body and flavors of winter squash and anadama bread. I suspect the hops are of the noble variety as they provide an accent of bitter herb. On the malt side are two-row, crystal and Munich—the Munich having been grown and malted locally. Stray Dog is similar, but in my opinion superior to that iconic craft brew, Samuel Adams' Boston Lager. Credit goes to the local malt.

Owner Tyler Guilmette comes down to Hadley in his pick-up truck to collect the Munich malt that makes up 25 percent of the grain bill. Brewmaster Jack's goal is to use 100 percent Valley Malt in the near future. One style that accomplishes just that is the Imperial IPA called Ambrewsia. The porter that Guilmette makes goes by the name Total Eclipse. This rich beer highlights the chocolate rye crafted by Valley Malt and contains 75 percent local grains.

Taste buds don't lie. One sip and its clear: native ingredients have flavor. That's one of the inescapable facts driving this market. If Valley Malt's product could not result in fresh and distinctive beers, they would likely be out of business. Instead, they are rapidly expanding production. To share in their accomplishments, they threw a party for a few fans of native beer, and more than 400 people showed up. "We were floored with how many people came." Andrea said.

On a more businesslike note, Valley Malt hosted a seminar for people interested in learning about this circular business model. The Farmer Brewer Winter Weekend sold out in advance and twenty people signed up on the waiting list. Then, Andrea went to Washington, DC to speak at the Craft Brewers Convention about the opportunity to create terroir in beer with local malt.

"It's cool we're seeing some success," she said. Cheers to that.

Field to Glass

Over the course of the twentieth century, an irreplaceable portion of fertile land in Massachusetts surrendered to developmental sprawl. One example of that is the town of Hadley. A big part of the story is dictated by Hadley's neighbors. Amherst is the next town to the east and home to the University of Massachusetts.

Beginning, ironically enough, as an agricultural college, the school expanded rapidly after World War II, creating a boomtown economy of shopping and housing that ate up fields faster than a plague of locusts. Not that the builders had much choice. It was all farmland. What else would people be doing with some of the most fertile land around?

We never thought we'd miss it, but now . . . the pastoral dream of fresh produce, natural meat, and eggs from hens that graze all day. Sounds good, right? Today, even as local food gains customer support, according to the Massachusetts Department of Agriculture, the Commonwealth continues to lose farmland, not only to the old pressures of housing and shopping, but now solar energy installations are converting farmland to electricity production.

Yet, for the small farms of the Northeast, signs of economic springtime are everywhere you look. The buy local movement continues to spend more money on local farm products every year. Even at supermarkets—bastion of the 2,000-mile lettuce—local produce is prominently displayed. Additionally, property values have dropped in the last five years, making land more affordable for agricultural preservation.

The business model that has accompanied this growth is Community Supported Agriculture or CSA, whereby farmers sell shares of the farm's yield to residents of the community. Not only does this direct-to-consumer sales program create allegiances between residents and farms, it allows a farmer to cover the expenses of the growing season in advance, breaking the old chokehold of debt-financed harvests. With a CSA, risk is shared among all the members. Without a CSA, many farmers would pay for seasonal expenses by taking out a loan, often using land as collateral. A poor harvest could result in the loss of arable land forever.

Now the CSA model has been applied to a new market. You guessed it—breweries. Valley Malt offers up harvest shares for $500 each. They found fifteen breweries in 2012 willing to advance the money to grow and malt grain. In this way, breweries share in the risk and reward of the harvest. And the risk is greater in New England than other places for reasons ranging from weather to grower inexperience. To meet the expanding market for local grain, some farmers have begun cultivating an unfamiliar crop and using share money to hedge against rookie mistakes.

Such was the case when researchers from the University of Massachusetts School of Agronomy visited the fields being cultivated for Brewery Supported Agriculture (BSA) shareholders. Forty-eight acres of two-row barley represented most of the 2012 BSA crop, with a potential yield of almost 2,000 pounds per acre and all of it being raised on western Massachusetts farms. On one eight-acre field, the researchers told Andrea that the crop suffered from a lack of nitrogen. Thanks to BSA money, she purchased and applied fertilizer that day. The farmer got a little help from an overnight rain that conveyed nutrients into the soil for the root system to take up. Like that, the crop was saved for the region's beer drinkers. Because of the success of BSA, that farm has one more cash crop to rely on.

Still, not everything can be controlled by the grower—rain, for example. In 2011, too much rain reduced the yield by 75 percent. A few days of rain at harvest time can cause the seed heads to become too heavy for the stalk to hold upright. Some may drop to the ground where the wet seeds sprout and set root. Others dip too low for the combine to collect, and others may simply rot.

On top of that difficulty, fusarium can be lurking in the field. Fusarium, a toxic fungus, may exist in every crop in small amounts. However, when the infection rate gets into double-digit percentages, the entire yield is considered unsafe for humans. If the infection levels climb much higher, the crop loses its potential as livestock feed. The farmer will still find a use for the raw material, but its value will be far below what was intended.

I asked Andrea if that kind of setback would discourage farmers enough to derail the new venture. She said that her growers responded to that poor harvest with a shrug and some knowing words: "That's farming."

They tried again in 2012 because, if not for perseverance, none of them would even be farmers. Sure enough, by many accounts, 2012 was a banner year for both yields and quality malting grain.

By sharing in the risk of low yields, brewers supported several western Massachusetts farms in a challenging year. One year later, they were rewarded with bounty. "We are finding that the grains coming from New England and New York are some of the nicest quality grains that we've seen," Andrea explains. "They have a freshness to them and flavor that you just can't get from the folks in the Midwest. It's been great to work with farmers who are eager to work with us because we're providing them a market to grow organic grains."

The brewer's nose makes a first impression with malt. Several brewers use the word "earthy" to describe the aromas and flavors from Valley Malt. Some have praised hints of fresh cut hay and golden honey. The pale ale malt I have in my kitchen consumes me with a homemade bread smell. Complex and unique, a real slice of the rural northeastern landscape expressed in a glass of beer.

Here are several special beers produced by BSA members:

- Blatant Brewery's first anniversary beer called BLATANTone is a Double IPA containing 55 percent locally grown pale malt and 15 percent locally grown rye malt.

- Cambridge Brewing Company makes a Valley Girl series, including the Valley Ghoul, a strong Scotch ale with pumpkins and local barley. Described as having a "super-rich malt character," this beer also contains brown sugar, molasses, and heather flowers.

- Ipswich Ale Brewery's spin-off brand, 5 Mile Ales, produces beer with at least one ingredient from within five miles of the brewery. Flavors include 5 Mile Stock Ale, dry-hopped with Cascade hops from their own hopyard and made with BSA barley malt. The 2013 spring release, Equinox Pale Ale, was made with barley and oats grown in Essex, Massachusetts. Prior to that, came the Hop Harvest, featuring hops grown in Ipswich and barley grown in Essex. To date, there have been six different releases so far.

- Night Shift Brewing's Viva Habanero is a rye ale brewed with agave nectar and aged on habanero peppers. True crafters, the folks at Night Shift offer tasting notes from each batch they make, including descriptions of flavors they are trying to create and alterations made to each batch.

- Notch Brewing Company makes Session Saison, and BSA Harvest, which is an American Farmhouse Ale.

- The People's Pint creates Star of the Valley and 100% local ale made with barley grown in Hadley and wheat grown in Belchertown, Massachusetts. Hops were grown in Northfield, Massachusetts and included Cascade and Nugget for a fine amber ale.

- Peak Organic Brewing Co. produces the Local Series and, according to owner Jon Cadoux, every beer coming out of Peak is now made with some portion of local ingredients.

- Throwback Brewery offers Hopstruck IPA, which they make with two-row, crystal, and Munich malts grown organically at Qualey Farms in Benedicta, Maine. Willamette hops were grown organically at Foothill Hops Farm and Home Brewing Shop in Madison County, New York.

- Wormtown puts Valley Malt in every batch, including the collaborative effort that resulted in Mass Appeal. BSA members involved were Cambridge Brewing, Night Shift, Idle Hands Craft Ales, and Mystic Brewery. These creative minds worked together, adding personality from each and using some local ingredients including malted wheat and a very special yeast strain cultivated at the Mystic Brewery fermentorium.

Other BSA members include Trillium Brewing, High Horse Brewing, and Pretty Things Beer & Ale Project.

BEER OF THE LAND

Among the farms with acreage reserved for BSA is Andrea and Christian's own Slow Tractor Farm. Having begun their career in malt by planting barley in their kitchen garden, it comes as no surprise that the Stanley's have increased the growing end of their business to more than forty acres under their own cultivation.

Most of the property they work is located in the neighboring town of Northampton on the western bank of the Connecticut River. This hip little city thrums with culture and Main Street commerce while, on the outskirts, some very old farms have slipped away. Yet, in at least one case, a large slice of farmland on the edge of survival was wholly embraced by the community.

Beginning as a small email listserv called "Grow Food Northampton," a group of like-minded residents managed to coalesce wide support around a campaign to save more than 100 acres of farmland for future agriculture. With a mission to improve community resilience by achieving food security, Grow Food Northampton wasn't about to stand by and allow another riverside farm to be lost.

At the same time, a large group of residents wanted the property for athletic fields and recreation. A recipe for civic meltdown? Not quite. According to many accounts, it was a heated debate and feathers were ruffled in both camps. Yet, with the city government setting the stage, the two sides hammered out a compromise that resulted in five soccer fields, two baseball diamonds, thirty-five acres of conservation land, and 121 acres of agricultural preservation. Now the old Bean and Allard farms that were so close to the end have opened a new chapter as the Northampton Community Farm.

At the ground breaking ceremony, a man sporting a green John Deere cap and a snow white beard stood up to speak. Introduced as Alan Everett, he once lived with extended family on this property. He said the Bean Farm was a good place to grow up because he learned many of life's lessons in the everyday activities. Having become a dairy farmer in nearby Williamsburg, Everett implored the young farmers of today to improve the land for future generations. Three entities share this responsibility for the Community Farm: Florence Community Garden, Crimson and Clover CSA, and Slow Tractor Farm.

In the spring of 2012, the Stanley's sowed their first crops in this field—fifteen acres with barley, ten with wheat and the rest with field beans to supply the nitrogen-fixing benefits of a legume. Also, Andrea notes, their combine can harvest the beans at the same setting used for grain. Rotation is important with any organic crop because plants tend to consume nutrients faster than they can be replenished. Some crops find their way into rotation in part because they offer something back to the soil. While legumes fix nitrogen for the use of succeeding crops, barley sends roots as much as six feet deep, creating a porous soil and drawing minerals and nutrients up to the top layer where the roots of most crops can have access. Winter grains also serve as runoff prevention during spring rains.

Andrea clearly enjoys thinking scientifically about the natural processes of farming and malting. She speaks at length with real interest on any facet of her varied work. "It's just exciting," she says. "I love the farming and growing aspect. Always something new to learn." Among what Andrea has grown herself are heirloom varieties. "It's a side geek passion of mine," she says. Hoping to find strains that are well adapted to the northeast winters, she searched the USDA Gene Bank for old varieties to bring back. Her focus had been on European two-row barley featuring low protein and plumpness. Since World War I, she explains, the Department of Agriculture has paid scientists to go around the world collecting genetic samples. "Your tax dollars at work." On the other hand, she says, "I'm just excited to be growing grains that haven't been planted in hundreds or sometimes thousands of years."

Breeding program on top of farm on top of malt house worked for the Stanley's on a smaller scale, but in the coming season, they've thrown their energy into expanded growing and malting. The decision has been made to leave the breeding to others. That's fine with Andrea. "There are barley breeders out there that know a hell of a lot more than I do," she says. Besides, with the market for malt the way it is, it makes more sense for her to focus solely on production.

"I didn't have time," she says. "There is still a need for a winter barley variety." On the other hand, recent winter seasons haven't been a problem. "We're having pretty awesome success with the winter barley we have. It's been three winters now."

As Valley Malt's capacity increases, so does their need for raw material and the acreage to produce it. Hundreds of acres of barley are contracted to Valley Malt and post-harvest purchases are made to supplement as needed. This is how the barley acreage breaks down: two-row winter barley is grown on 105 acres in New York, eighty-three acres in Massachusetts, and five acres in Connecticut; two-row spring barley is grown on thirty acres in New York, fifteen acres in Massachusetts, and 100 acres in Maine; and six-row spring barley is grown on forty acres in New York.

WHERE THE FARMS ARE

One grower taking advantage of this new market is Upinngil Farm, with five acres of malting grains in Gill, Massachusetts. A town of about 1,500 inhabitants, Gill sits on an elbow of the Connecticut River where the water's path takes a sudden westward turn, a place with evidence of man's presence from over 10,000 years ago. The first European colonists came this way prior to 1676 and settled on rich land.

Today more than 40 percent of the land is used for agriculture, almost 4,000 acres. More than 100 of those belong to Upinngil's father and daughter team, Clifford and Sorrel Hatch. Upinngil specializes in raw milk, but also offers pick-your-own berries, farmstead cheese, and eggs, all raised on fields that have been under the care of a farmer for more than 300 years. Likewise, the Hatch family itself is said to have roots in New England farming that go back to the first half of the 1600s.

For a while Cliff pursued a career as a chef, but farming called him back. "I grew up on a farm. It's all I ever really wanted to do." Like father, like daughter. Sorrel grew up on her father's farm starting an egg business when she was only five years old. Having obtained a degree in etymology from Cornell University, she spurned post-graduate opportunities for a return to Gill and the farm.

Growing up, Sorrel recalls following her father around the farm and learning how to use garden tools and identify plants. Sorrel believes her farm helps build a healthy community based on healthy land. She says the disconnect between the general public and its food source leads to production methods that degrade the soil ecosystem.

On a gray February day with cold rain threatening, Sorrel has her hands in bread dough when I call. "I do a lot of baking," she explains. And why not? After all, her farm grows twenty-five acres of grain, most of it for flour, and teams up with Cold Spring Farm to do business as Gill Organic Grains.

Upinngil didn't dabble in grain farming until a nearby bakery asked if they could supply wheat. That was in 2005. The Hatch's have learned a lot since then. Sorrel says the main problem with grain farming in her neck of the woods is the harvest. "It grows just fine," she says. But without a nice, solid, hot and dry week when the grain is mature, the harvest is likely to suffer losses. "It's tricky at the end of July when the winter wheat and rye come in," she says. That time of year tends to be humid with frequent showers, although in New England, the weather is anything but predictable.

"Last year's dry weather produced an excellent quality harvest," says Cliff. "Everything I brought in was good. Weather has a lot to do with it around here. I grew for Valley Malt a particular variety of barley they wanted and they provided the seed. Five to six acres last year and we got a few tons out of it." He noted that Valley Malt makes a trade-off with the malting grain they select, opting for flavor over harvest weight. Cliff said, "Not a lot of quantity, I thought. Not something I'd grow myself."

The Hatches have not found it difficult to sell their grain harvest. "We've got an interested market willing to pay for a local product," Sorrel says. At the same time, should the crop be less than ideal, "We've got livestock to feed it to. I raise chickens. Some years I might have a lot of chickens depending how the crop does. Everything goes to use one way or another."

Gill Organic Grains Harvest

Upinngil's mission sets the goals of being environmentally sound, connecting people to the land where their food grows, and using sustainable methods. I ask Cliff what it means to farm sustainably. He says, "It means I do things as cheaply as possible." Then he laughs. "Everything is recycled. Try to keep the system as closed as possible. Don't buy in anything if I can get away with it. I still wind up paying people a lot of money for some things." But when he does, he always tries harder to fill that need on site. Experience has been his teacher. "I used to buy in straw for my strawberries," he says cheerily, "and I got weeds I'll never get rid of. I got enough problems without going out and asking for them."

For a cover crop, he says, winter grains are sown. Working them into rotation with other crops makes the most sense. "You can't keep growing grains in the same place," he says. "After a while, you have to seed for hay and alfalfa to build it back. It all works together—cows, chickens, crop rotations. It all works together." Seed is something worth buying in, he says, because it is certified to be disease-free. On the other hand, he adds, "When I have something that does real well, I'll save the seed because it's well suited to the muggy climate." In that way, he says, the plant's selective adaptation can be used to his benefit. "All those genes are being turned on and off," he explains. But even with seed that does well one season, there are no guarantees the next. I ask him how much of the outcome the farmer can control. His answer: "None of it."

Still, I reason, it must be rewarding to finally taste beer made with grain he grew himself. Well, not so much. "I have to admit I'm a nihilist when it comes to beer," Cliff says. "I'll have a Corona as soon as any of these others. Mostly I'm a wine drinker and I grow my own grapes for making wine." While Cliff enjoys the terroir in his wine glass, beer fans get the same essence with brews like Element Brewing's Spring Interval release. Called Vernal, this beer uses malt organically grown in Gill.

A Notch in My Belt

Friday evening, late October, my good friend Jeff brings a mixed six-pack of Notch Session to share. This is exciting news since I know they use Valley Malt and I have never tried any of the Notch flavors before. In my hand, a Saison, brewed with Massachusetts-grown and malted wheat. This farmhouse ale possesses an uncultivated yeasty aroma filled with spice notes. Pouring out a clean straw color with a very generous champagne head, the effervescence comes over the top of the mug releasing intense citrus notes and bready comfort. The gentle bite of wheat malt accentuates the dry finish and highlights another citrus blast, a cross between orange and grapefruit—almost pucker dry. Strangely, this makes me think of that old pizza place standby: dry orange soda from the days before everything tasted like corn syrup.

Coming in at 3.8 percent alcohol, I could gulp down two or three of these before I have a handle on its real character. So often a twelve-ounce bottle leaves me unsatisfied. Yet, like the dwindling daylight hours, I am forced to savor and find myself swishing the suds between tongue and teeth.

According to the Notch website, their Saison is "brewed to the original saison strength. This is the classic farmhouse beer. Originally brewed by farmers to slake the thirst of seasonal workers (*les saisonniers*), this refreshing beer had a lower alcohol content that is not often seen in today's modern Saison. Notch returns the Saison to its roots, not only in alcohol content, but by using local ingredients much like the Belgian farmers."

If you think about it, working in the sun all day with only beer to drink would be inhumane if a two-beer buzz made you want to laugh and dance. Obviously, beer like this would be the only way to accomplish this drinking and working daily marathon, as the French farmers and many others of the pre-nineteenth century were reputed to have done. Lower alcohol, longer hours of drinking, thus the name: Session.

Aside from being a tasty little brew, this Notch Session does a good job sparking lively conversations. The Saison came out in March and is hardly at its freshest seven months later. The funky Belgian yeast, however, seems to have kept working right along, as the lively flavor attests. This is a great way to preserve the local harvest.

Terrain of an Ale

Back in Northampton, Suzanne and I escorted our two five-foot plus children into a brick oven joint called Pizza Paradiso where the menu states local ingredients are included "whenever possible." On this day in mid-February, however, the only off-season ingredient to be found has been preserved in liquid form and stored in a keg.

Peak Organic Amber Ale arrived in our waitress's sure hands. Holding the glass out of the light, I could see only rusty brown, but in front of the window, filtered light gleamed through the deep brown beer to reveal an iridescent amber jewel. As I gazed into the trippy reflection of the window through the pint glass, I heard Suzanne say, "Mmm."

A little off-white foam on her lip drained into her mouth and I had to stop looking and start drinking. Once again, a discovery of flavors heightened my senses. Beer. Was it Benjamin Franklin who was credited with observing that beer is proof that God loves us and wants us to be happy?

This was simply the best beer I'd ever had. Full disclosure requires me to say that it was also the first beer of the day. For me, first of the day is always the best. And gone too quickly. Yet, thanks to an attentive waitress, my second beer landed on the table with one swig still left in the first. Next to helping myself to the tap, this is as good as it gets. Adding to my appreciation is the strong memory of when all beer came in only one color, yellow. Mass-marketing and mass-consumption had driven the market to a product that was cheap to manufacture and able to last on shelves across the globe.

Changes on the beer terrain over much of the continent have been revolutionary. Now, places like this pizza joint offer ten drafts of craft beer and a dozen or so bottle options. The variety ranges from light yellow rye to black barley stouts and many shades in between. Once upon a time, not so long ago, craft beer did not exist. For most of the eight decades since the repeal of Prohibition, virtually all beer came in only one yellowish color with dominant flavors of fermented rice or corn extract. Hops? Compared to today's standards, there weren't any hop flavors. Bland enough to be inoffensive for most palates, this canned product comes in a few different labels, but inside are just copycats of each other.

This one-size-fits-all beer market couldn't possibly be supplied by local farm communities. Instead, factory beer acquires ingredients on the commodity market, putting grain growers at the mercy of corporate hierarchies, consolidation, and the drive for quarterly shareholder profits. To assure the long distance marketability of this omnipresent product, the beer is heated after it's done fermenting, to kill any residual yeast, and filtered to remove most of the nutrient content that might feed hardy microbial life. This kind of beer is no longer enjoyed as a food itself, but many decades ago it became, essentially, sterilized junk food. And for a lifetime, as citizens morphed into consumers and communities transformed from actual to virtual, it seemed the change in the beer terrain would be permanent.

The number of craft brewers, however, has grown steadily along with market share for more than ten years now. In the past two years, craft beer growth, according to the Brewers Association has been in the double digits nationwide. Every time a brewery opens or expands, farmers get a potential customer.

The epicenter of this movement for New England may be debatable, but my vote goes to Portland, Maine. Ten brewing facilities call this city on the Gulf of Maine home: Allagash Brewing Company, Bull Jagger Brewing Company, Bunker Brewing Company, D.L. Geary Brewing Company, Gritty McDuff's Brewing Company, Maine Beer Company, Rising Tide Brewing Company, Sebago Brewing Company, Sea Dog Brewing Company, and Shipyard Brewing Company. Furthermore, the Shipyard facility produces beer for Casco Bay Brewing Company, Vermont's Woodstock Inn, and for Peak Organic. That's a lot of beer in a small city.

The first colonial dwellings here were established on the shores of the harbor in 1633 for the purposes of fishing and trading. In the bloody year of 1676, the Abenaki Tribe wiped out the entire village. Soon resettled, the Indians were back in 1690 with assistance from French forces. Again, the English colonists were defeated and driven off. Rebuilt in 1713, the growing seaport was destroyed once more in 1775. This time it was the British themselves, punishing a town unsure of its allegiances at the advent of the Revolution. After a day-long bombardment by the Royal Navy, Portland's inhabitants had become hardened rebels. That streak came back to life about seventy-five years later.

Many cities built around the docks have a hardworking and hard drinking population. Portland has never been an exception to this rule. However, the rest of the state felt differently about alcohol during the middle of the nineteenth century. In fact, in 1851, Maine banned all non-medicinal alcohol. A short while later, the thirsty citizens of Portland protested in the streets. Known as the Rum Riot, one protester died when the militia opened fire on an unruly mob. That liquor loving martyr did not die in vain. By 1858, the beer flowed freely once again after repeal of what had nationally been called the Maine Law.

Meanwhile, in the rest of New England's largest state, timber, granite, and farm crops became the mainstay ways of life, while fishing dominated the coastline. Wild blueberries, potatoes, dairy, and even hops were all part of the mix that nourished the population. Of all the occupations that dominated Maine's history—lumberjack, quarryman, fisherman, trader, and farmer—one remained most important to those who ventured from their homes to inhabit these shores and forests.

According to historian and Maine native Alan Taylor, farming was the point. After all, why would the settlers live such a difficult and dangerous life carving farmland from the forest? Because it was the only way to be independent. Day laborers and tenant farmers had nothing at the end of the line. However, with a farm of its own, one generation could improve the lot of the next. The path to the good life for anyone starting with little more than a few tools and animals, lay in owning and working your own land.

Of the crops Mainers used to support themselves, dairy and hops have faced the most decline over the years. But since 2007, one Portland beer company has been determined to develop a market for local and organically grown hops and grain. Jon Cadoux, who started Peak Organic Brewing with his brother Mike, describes their commitment to local growers. "Really at Peak, our reason for being is stimulating and supporting the resurgence of hop growing and barley growing throughout the region."

Today, most worthwhile spirit shops in the Northeast carry Peak Organic. Only five years ago, Cadoux says, "We started out extraordinarily small. Now, every year, five or six organic farms come on line for us. Like any business, growers need to see that there is someone out there to buy what they produce." Peak Organic is determined to be part of that market. "Every single beer Peak makes has some locally grown product in it."

At least part of Peak's support for local farms stems from the lack of organic brewing ingredients in the global supply, especially when it comes to hops. In the northwestern United States, where the vast majority of domestic hops are grown, the production at most farms is counted in the hundreds of acres. Petroleum-based fertilizers and synthetic pesticides dominate the cultivation of hops. "Three or four years ago," Cadoux recalls, "it was really hard putting it together." Working locally, Peak is able to increase their supply of organic ingredients to further align with their mission.

The drive to stay local has other benefits for Peak. Some brewers have customers and suppliers. Others, like Peak, who get ingredients from nearby farms, find themselves knitted into a community wholecloth. From farmer to brewer to maltster to customer, all Jon Cadoux sees are friends in this network of people who live and work within the region. For him, that's the most satisfying part of what's been created with Peak. "We love having relationships with people who have the same philosophy we do."

Like Ben Roesch of Wormtown, the Cadoux brothers have to venture out into farm country assuring their supplies. "We spend an enormous amount of time on that," Jon says. "Mostly networking with farmers. We shake hands. Our word is good. If you grow it organically, we'll buy everything you grow. From the end of July to mid-September, we're on farms full-time, especially on the hop side helping with harvest. Growers have these fantastic hops that we're unable to get without handpicking." But handpicking is very labor intensive.

Fortunately, it's a job that can be done while drinking beer. So, to get the harvest in, he throws a party. "It's a pickin' party," he says. "We drink beer and pick hops. Right now I'm trying to get another team for this year. We get bar managers, distributors. We try to get people involved. Then we descend, a whole bunch of people, onto a farm and pick 200 to 300 plants. It takes an absolute ton of time. Farmers can't pick them on their own and, you know, helping them feels good."

Jon elaborates on the math involved. "It takes forty-five minutes to handpick one pound and there are machines that do it in thirty seconds. The quality has pretty much always been there. Supply is the bottle neck. We need the infrastructure to catch up."

Until harvest machines begin to find a spot in barns on these farms, the Cadouxs will be out there getting the crop in the old-fashioned way. That's a lot of extra work that most brewery owners don't bother to do. But Jon wouldn't have it any other way. He stresses the importance of local farms being economically viable.

"There is absolutely no doubt that is critical," he says. "Once farming becomes commoditized, it moves away." He adds that buying local equates with "keeping people employed and the local economy thriving, keeping our region thriving. We're going to have to return to growing things and making things. The old school values are the future of our region and it's really important to the intellect and on an emotional level."

To the Cadouxs, local and organic feel like the right things do and that feels good. "It's a blast for me," Jon says. "That connection to the farm is a real important piece of our business. I think when it comes to quality of life, this is a pretty amazing experience. For us at Peak, we really value working closely with our farmers."

Peak organic is just getting warmed up. "Our goal is to massively increase supply," Jon says. "One hundred percent is what we're running towards. It's moving in that direction. There's an infrastructure gap in post-harvest technology, but," he adds, ever the optimist, "if there is a demand, then that gap will be bridged. It's going to happen, but it takes time."

He cites Valley Malt as an example of how the enterprising spirit looks at those holes in the market and sees possibilities. "People like Andrea see the opportunity to make that connection," he says. "Valley Malt is a great partner. They're doing a wonderful job of being the link between growers and brewers. They've been instrumental in spearheading local grain growing for beer in the Northeast and they're just great folks."

Yet, Peak did not begin this buy local and organic stuff to make friends. As Mike Cadoux says, "For us, the important thing was mostly the taste. When we brewed our first organic beer we thought it was just crisper and cleaner. I think it makes sense that products that were cared for a little better would taste a little better." For that reason, local and fresh is the way to go. Jon adds, "We love seeing a lot of barley and hop production shifting back to the Northeast. We think these crops are absolutely as good if not better than anything else growing in the world."

On their website, Peak recognizes several of the local farmers who provide them with ingredients. To showcase these ingredients, they released a series of four beers all using the same recipe, but made with ingredients from different states: Maine, Vermont, New York, and Massachusetts. The obvious differences in flavor were derived from the source of the ingredients.

"That project was amazing," Jon says. "Experiencing beers so wildly different, but made with essentially the same recipe, really brought out the terroir of the different regions." While the recipe aimed for a hoppy experience, the results tended to accentuate unique favors in the malt.

"These local grains have an heirloom quality," Jon says. "The grains really shine. You can definitely tell the differences on both the grain and the hop sides of the beer."

Here's a breakdown of the flavor profiles: Massachusetts resulted in a golden orange glass with tints of light brown. Hazy with a white head, a floral aroma gives way to black tea and rainy pine forests. Add to that just a touch of butterscotch, and you get the idea. A good full malt flavor combines with subdued bitterness that grows at the finish.

Vermont differs in color. It's darker and creamier, and the hops are slightly less noticeable.

The Maine version has a rubiness to the color, and a somewhat smaller head. A fruity aroma weaves into that evergreen layer with a punch of citrus. Malt provides a light toastiness. The bitter finish here is the cleanest.

The New Yorker among this crowd is the most boisterous. A bright, almost red pour leaves a foamy white head and emits berries, vanilla, and maybe honey. A medium to full body releases layers of flavor that doesn't deviate from those in the aroma. Fruitiness, whole grain bread, and caramel/vanilla all swept clean by a mild and pleasing bitter finish.

Which one is the best? Whichever one I have in my mouth. After I try them all, I just want to start over again.

Jon's experience with the different sub-regions of the Northeast has revealed that a Cascade hop grown in Maine will have obvious differences in characteristics from one grown in Vermont. Mike points out that Peak's goals are lofty—to make some of the best beer in the world. To accomplish that, he says, the best ingredients are required. The Local Series showed the world class nature of the Northeast's beer ingredients. Now Peak needs to get more of them, and fine tune recipes that emphasize the qualities of the local beer terrain.

The Rising Tide of Independence

Independence Day is near as I sit on the wet sand in York, Maine. The cold gulf water laps at my legs as I work a crude knife into the joint of an oyster shell. To my left is a plastic bag with eleven more of these tasty morsels, all harvested in these waters. Earlier today, we stopped by Harbor Fish Market in Portland and picked them out one by one to enjoy right now. Yes, it's summer. Yes, the oysters are not considered at their peak, but I am hoping the contents of this shell, when I finally open it, will reveal something tantalizing.

To my left is a red plastic cup of the kind available at keg parties. In the cup is the perfect summer beer—a pale ale made with locally grown and malted rye. Having driven through Wells a few days ago, we had to stop in at Tully's Beer & Wine to see the vast array of Maine beers. With an employee who looked too young to drink schooling me in the details of each brew, it took no time at all to select Daymark by Rising Tide Brewing Company.

That afternoon we swam at Crescent Beach on Cape Elizabeth. Chased back to the car by thunderheads, we headed to the city for fireworks over the esplanade. Really, the natural light show outdid the man-made one, but they were both chest-thumping loud. I drank a few beers the night before, but had saved one for this moment. Suzanne sat next to me in a beach chair, red cup between her knees, as she stared off after the children in the waves.

At last, the oyster gives up the fight and I pry the pearly shell open with great care so as to keep from spilling the sweet brine. The truth in the folk wisdom that admonishes us to eat oysters only in months that contain the letter 'R' is revealed to me in this specimen. Instead of a gunmetal gray, plump, and clean looking scoop of bivalve meat, this oyster is milky and somewhat flat. Scuttling my plan to offer Suzanne the first one, I feel I must be the guinea pig here. Crossing my fingers, I hold the half-shell to my bottom lip and open wide.

Not bad. Creamy, but still a distinct brininess, and that minerally sweet oyster flavor that I love. Then, I swallow some beer. Now it's coming together. The crispness of the rye cuts the creaminess like a dry wine cuts through strong cheese. This is the ideal accompaniment. Beer and oysters and waves and wind. Before the rivers of Maine poured out from the land into the tidal flats and estuaries inhabited by these oysters, the same water fell on the rye in this beer, grown on a small family farm not far from where I sit.

Gazing out over the sea, the endless heaving and lapping of waves bears a resemblance to a field of ripe grain swaying in the gentle summer breeze.

One by one, the oysters surrender their flavor. Sip by sip, I lose the strain and tension of a modern world that often seems to spiral away from its core. Right now, I am here, immersed in the sea and sand, coated by the sun and filled with the bounty that surrounds me.

FARMING ON A STRING

For some people, it all starts with homebrewing. The small investment of a homebrew kit is often undertaken for the reasons of saving money on beer, copying favorite styles, and taking ownership over the creative process. In Steve Prouty's case, it's all about having a good time. "Hey, the sun sets every day," he says. "Gotta have some fun."

Many homebrewers like their fun so much, they take the next step—growing their own ingredients. Hops are especially rewarding. Readily available in homebrew shops and from online suppliers, hop rhizomes are twig-like sections of the plant that grow underground. Anyone with a flag pole or a sunny exterior wall for the vines to climb can plant a few rhizomes and expect a perennial crop of fresh hops in their beer at harvest time.

For Prouty, a similar scenario played out, but as someone who raises crops on 400 acres, his hopyard is more than a hobby. Prouty calls it a test plot. At Clover Hill Farm in Hardwick, Massachusetts, he and his son work land that has been in their family for five generations, beginning in 1888. These days their main crops are feed hay and cranberries. One reason for that success is their willingness to innovate. Already selling cranberries to wineries and brewers, he thought he'd diversify his products for that market by planting hops.

Around the same time, he learned of a hop farming feasibility study conducted for the University of Vermont in 2010. Delivered at the first annual conference on growing hops in the Northeast, the report states:

> "There is sufficient demand from the brewing community to support a minimum of 100 acres in production. There is sufficient price point elasticity to afford producers an ability to generate a profit, and a reasonable timeframe for return on investment. The information, technology, and equipment now exist for smaller scale, one to ten-acre commercial hop operations. Aside from potential limitations of topsoil depth to bedrock, New England's growing climate and conditions are well suited to hop production."

That market analysis set the farming community to work building hop trellises and ordering rhizomes. Prouty is among those who have been convinced by the university to give hop farming a try. "They're the ones that got us going," he says. UVM's stated goal is to expand income opportunities for farmers. So far, the results have been mixed.

Prouty planted a third of an acre with 400 plants of four varieties: Cascade, Willamette, Nugget and Chinook. Of those Chinook was most productive in 2012. That first harvest yielded only about sixty pounds, but hop plants take at least three years to fully mature. UVM Soil and Crop Scientist Heather Darby says the threshold for a profitable hop crop is 1,500 pounds of dried hops per acre. Fresh hop weight is four times that of dry.

"You don't expect to see much in the first two years," Prouty explains. To be profitable hop farming requires specialized equipment including harvester, bailer and oast for drying. Today, Prouty is yet to make that leap. In fact, he has given up on harvesting all his hops. Instead, he takes a very low maintenance approach that allows him his personal hops for brewing and offers a pick your own fresh hops experience for other homebrewers.

At the same time, he can see there are brewers who want more local hops than are currently in production. "Right now, the market is wide open. There aren't a whole lot of hops being grown in Massachusetts. Last year Wormtown Brewery bought everything we had." Getting the crop into a brewer's hands without using a mechanical harvester turned out to be a lot of fun. "I find every friend I can think of who will still be my friend at the end of the day," Prouty says. "Then I buy a shitload of beer and we go at it. We pick." A few weeks later, about twenty-five miles to the east, taps flowed with MassWhole Hop Harvest. Prouty found the experience gratifying. "We went in and drank most of what they had," he says with a laugh.

The Hop Harvest Ale, made with Massachusetts-raised grains processed at Valley Malt, weighed in at 5.8 percent alcohol and stood tall with sixty International Bittering Units, the scale used for hop bitterness of any given beer. Not the ninety IBU's of west coast double IPA's, for certain. This was not a loud flavor. Not a cheek puckering, tongue sticking, pine resiny zing from the Great Northwest. This drink was a milder, somewhat more approachable ale of the Northeast. Added to the Chinook hops from Clover Hill were Magnum and Cascade from Four Star Farms in Northfield. Geographic influences were accentuated by the floral quality of hops fresh off the vine.

Memories and images are often stirred by aromas that connect different places and times. This glass reminded me of the hiking trails of the Rock House Reservation near my home in West Brookfield. Something about that fresh forest smell and the robust oxygenated air arose from that hop blend. There was a combination of created flavors from the New England woodlands and grassy meadows, punctuated by a glimmer of lemon sorrel. If the way people describe flavors and aromas of beer and wine seems overly dramatic, it's only because the writer is teasing out subtle cues and hints from a complex and unique experience. It's no wonder that ancient civilizations viewed beer as a sort of magical way to get in touch with the spirit world. The experience is not easily related in words. This Hop Harvest is no different.

Hops are the movie stars of the beer world. They show up, usually at the end of a long process, jump in the pool for a spell, and come up first on everyone's tongue. Hot commodities, new hop farms are popping up from Minnesota to the Rhode Island coast.

The farmers of the Northeast face numerous special challenges. "Climate issues," Prouty laments. Springs and summers are often humid here and mildew can develop, a deadly disease that could spell disaster for the season, as well as the end of a perennial crop's fifteen years of life expectancy. Then there are insects, the potato leafhopper, the Eastern Comma butterfly, Japanese beetles and mites. To Prouty, that's part of doing business. "We grow crops full-time," he says. "It's how we make our living. Hops are like any other crop. Takes a year or two of screwing up before you figure it out."

HOPYARDS OF YORE

Beer is as old as civilization itself. Among our first written records are beer recipes. This ancient fermentation had a lot in common with beer of the modern world. Chiefly composed of malted grains and water, a wild predecessor of today's cultivated brewers' yeast transformed the pasty mix into a satisfying drink. After a while brewers began stirring in culinary herbs like rosemary and sage, but not hops.

When people think of beer today, malt and hops are both considered essential. That's why it can come as a surprise to learn that beer was around for 9,000 years before man discovered how to use hops to flavor and preserve their brews. The earliest written evidence of hops used in beer isn't until the twelfth century. The story goes that brewers were mixing potent herbal medicines with their beer for more than flavoring and preservative purposes. For example, Wormwood, responsible for the psychotropic effects of absinthe, was commonly used. During the Roman Empire, the Pict peoples of Scotland were said to drink heather beer before battle. The drink got credit for making them unbeatable. Increases in energy and courage were likely caused by a fungal growth found in the little heather flowers. Alcohol itself tends to dull the senses and reduce levels of fear.

Authorities in the Middle Ages didn't want their serfs to be fearless and uncontrollable. One herb known for its drowsy and sedating effects promised a more docile population. Hops not only can cause yawns, but filled with a molecular component that is used by the body to produce estrogen, that quintessential female hormone, they also cause the male gender to . . . well, let's just say that men are a little less rough around the edges when they consume it.

Royalty had their motives for restricting beer ingredients via rules such as the 1516 German purity law which allowed for the use of only water, barley, and hops. Because hops taste so darn pleasingly good, it's easy to see why the peasants accepted these decrees. It should be noted that Belgium was the lone European holdout, where the liberal use of a wide variety of ingredients remains in practice. There, brewers saved for the modern world the old ways of adding herbs and spices and whatever else will enhance the final product.

By the time Europeans began colonizing the northeast coast of America, hops were important enough to establish as early as 1629. By the end of the eighteenth century, Massachusetts farmers were exporting thousands of pounds of hops and Massachusetts had a reputation for quality hops among brewers. Hop growing succeeded here in spite of unpredictable harvests. As is all too clear to modern hop farmers, the plant is very attractive to insects and rainy seasons can spell doom.

According to a report published on the Old Sturbridge Village website, almost all of the hops crop grew in three adjacent towns: Tewksbury, Wilmington, and Billerica. Around the turn of the century, hop farming spread to Bedford, New Hampshire. Farmers from here dominated the hop market in the United States for decades to come. But the westward creep of the hop bine continued.

Next were Vermont and New York. First, Vermont passed Mass-achusetts and New Hampshire to become the biggest producer. Then farmers in upstate New York took the honors in 1850 and didn't look back for more than sixty years, producing three to four times the volume of New England growers.

These early hop farmers knew that an effective method for preserving the harvest was the top priority. Only so much can be used fresh. As a harvest time treat, a wet hopped beer is fine, but to brew all year long, hops must be dried in such a way as to preserve as much of the flavor as possible.

The hop industry of the Northeast continued strong right up until Prohibition destroyed the market. By the time the people could legally purchase beer again, hops production in the northwest grew beyond anything the east coast had been able to do. Thanks to larger tracts of land and technological advances that made large-scale hop farming feasible, as well as a drier climate and fewer diseases, places to the east of the Cascade mountain range took over the industry and never looked back.

They did, however, send back some of their root stock. In 2010, Heather Darby planted it in Vermont soil. This hopyard is not for commercial production, though. Darby, a biologist at the University of Vermont, wants to find out which hop varieties grow best in the Northeast using organic pest control and soil building methods. She has twenty-four varieties in trial a hopyard.

"The first year looked very promising," she says. "We're looking to get 1,000 to 2,000 pounds per acre, dried. The first year we got 300 pounds and we thought, 'pretty good.' This year was 500 pounds per acre from the best yielding plant." That's not a lot of progress and double the harvest is needed to meet the minimum goal of 1,000 dry pounds by next year.

Still, because of the life expectancy of the perennial hop plant, the crop has time to repay the investment. While it is still early in the trials, Darby has a few varieties she thinks are well suited to the Northeast.

"You're going to want reasonable disease resistance and high yield," she says. Given that, she recommends Cascade, for starters. Perhaps the most popular hop in the country, Cascade has spicy, floral, grapefruit characteristics that are found in the aromas and flavors of this hop. An offspring of English Fuggle and a Russian variety, Cascade was bred by the USDA and entered the marketplace in the 1970s. It is the signature hop of west coast style IPA's, which are very popular these days, making this variety a good one to grow.

The brewer can use hops in a variety of ways. Added at the beginning of the process, the hop oils and other compounds break down over the period of boiling and provide a bitterness that balances malt sugars left unfermented. Added to the end of the boil, the oils break down less and flavors of fruit, herbs, and indefinable earthy tones are created. Sometimes hops are added after the beer is cooled. These late additions leave the essential oils intact and strongly influence the aroma. Hops can be used at any point during the brewing process and each stage of addition and each variety of hop will feather another layer into the drinking. Cascade is commonly used at every step of the brew.

Nugget is another Darby recommendation. A cultivar used most often for bittering, Nugget was bred from Brewer's Gold crossed with several others, including some unknown hop variety. Yields are heavy and aroma properties are strong and herbal. She suggests Newport as a bittering variety that gives the northeast grower a chance at success. This hop is only ten years old and was bred to resist mildew. "It's still a little too early to tell which would be best long term," Darby cautions.

Another variety farmers say works well is Chinook, a multi-purpose strain good for bittering, flavoring, and aroma additions. Used in everything from IPAs to stout, this hop brings a full-bodied, spicy, pine-tinted aroma. Some growers report having good harvests of Centennial. With strong alpha acids and desirable flavor properties, this is another popular choice.

Darby says that the tentative success of UVM's field does not mean farmers won't do well. On the contrary, she thinks what is being learned at UVM helps farmers make good decisions. "I feel like our job is to do everything wrong," she says. "Farmers getting in now have an advantage because we've made those mistakes, but it's a perennial and the worst thing is getting off on the wrong foot. If the crop is not well established, you'll pay for it later."

Among growers and beer enthusiasts, there is no lack of interest in northeast hops. Darby reports 200 people attended each of two annual conferences with others having to be turned away. She hears from growers how important it is to have a resource in UVM. "Farmers have been saying, 'I always wanted to grow hops but I had nowhere to go for help.'" UVM funds its research with grants and has gotten support from the Vermont Craft Brewers Guild.

To grow hops, the farmers need to know how the crop grows, what kind of soil is best, how to handle pests, and so forth. The first thing to think about is that hops want to grow straight up. Farmers have to build trellises upwards of twenty feet high with a horizontal cable running the length of the row from which vertical lines are dropped to the plants below. Technically called bines rather than vines, the plant must be trained to the string in a corkscrew fashion. They pop through the ground in early spring and grow rapidly through June before spending their energy producing flowers, or cones. The cones are harvested in the Northeast anywhere from late July to late September, depending on variety and weather. What happens next is where northeast hop farmers will need to focus their resources in the coming years.

The harvest will need to be mechanized and, perhaps more importantly, the harvest needs to be better preserved. Everyone I spoke with—from brewers to growers to scientists—recognizes the need for preserving the volatile flavors in the harvest. In the northwest, the cones are dried, then vacuum-sealed either as whole leaf or pellets. Even then, they must be refrigerated. After all that, the decomposition is merely slowed, not halted. Farmers just starting out with hops tend to use inexact drying methods, laying the crop out on screens and setting aside in a barn, often with a fan circulating air. This process is obviously dependent on outside humidity levels and is tested for completion by touch and feel. In the major hop growing regions, the drying is done in a controlled environment and completion is detected by scientific measurements.

One noticeable difference between West Coast hops and East Coast hops has been the capacity to provide bitterness. Darby says, "We've done some tests and taste tests. They are different. My perspective is they are like grapes. The terroir is not bad, just different." Same goes for flavors. "I've heard brewers say ours are grassier, not as strong. It just requires creativity . . . new beers to express the differences. We have to learn how to work with it. It's only been a couple years. It's the same thing with grains—ours will never be like Kansas grain." But, she says, the effort to create a local brewer supply market will work "if we take advantage of what we have and craft beer that suits its strengths. We have a lot to learn still."

Darby started her trial hopyard with the intention of developing organic methods in response to a change in the rules for beer labeling, which requires all beer with an organic label to use only organic hops. Still, Darby feels the most effective pest control methods involve a mix of organic and synthetic controls. She says it's important to encourage beneficial predatory insects. One way to do this is to avoid killing them. She points out that when an organic insecticide is used, it may impact all the bugs in the immediate environment, including the ones that are helping to clear out the pests. Synthetic poisons, she says, can be more precisely targeted. This is the middle route taken by the leader among Massachusetts hop growers.

Star of the Field

Adaptability is the hallmark of any long lasting farm in the Northeast. For Gene L'Etoile, the time to diversify his turf farm is here. After four years of testing and slow expansion, his Four Star Farms in Northfield, Massachusetts put 4,000 new hops plants in the ground. Added to the 2,000 plants installed the previous year, this increase makes Four Star one of the leading area growers. "Once we get those plants in," L'Etoile told me last winter, "I'd say we'll be the biggest around here."

Joining his Cascade, Magnum, Willamette, Mt. Hood, Kent Goldings and Nugget are Sterling (a hybrid with Saaz character), Centennial, and New Zealand's cultivar AlphAroma. The 400 plants from the first year, now fully mature, have provided enough evidence of success to convince L'Etoile to ramp up his operation. But in his understated and somewhat clipped way of speaking, he says, "The harvest was decent—several hundred pounds."

Those hops went on to find their way into beers at Northampton Brewery, Jack's Abbey Brewing, and Berkshire Brewing Company. "It was all sold shortly after harvest," L'Etoile says. In beers such as The People's Pint's Star of the Valley, the farm even found its way into the name. Joining the hops in many beers is Four Star's wheat crop, making this one of the few operations to provide both major farm ingredients brewers need.

Considering all the well known obstacles to successful northeast hop farming, L'Etoile's investment represents some optimism. More than that, however, the step-by-step expansion of his hop crop represents a measured approach that has demonstrated the opportunity to establish a long-term industry.

Plants are one thing, and certainly have their price tag, but equipment costs are where things get serious. L'Etoile knows this better than anyone. He's already purchased his own harvester, a German model that had been in use since 1980 before it arrived at his farm. Expensive machines are a commitment, not just the purchase, but the maintenance and repairs that go along with it.

Again, L'Etoile didn't jump in without testing the waters. A few years ago, he was the first farmer to try out a prototype mobile harvester designed and built for UVM in partnership with MDAR. The idea is to have a machine that can be shared among area hop farmers in the model of grain harvesters of the Midwest. L'Etoile says of the machine, "It worked well. Had some bugs to work out."

Last year it was fine-tuned again. Now the plans are available on the UVM hops site. Darby says she's heard from new hop farmers in different part of the country that have used the free design and made their own versions. The value to the farmer can't be understated.

"It's a chore to pick by hand," L'Etoile says. "One hour per pound. It sells for about $10." In three days with the harvester, Four Star Farms picked 550 pounds of wet hops, working eight hours a day. That's an increase in output of twenty-two times what could be picked by hand. Harvesters are critical to making hop growing economically viable.

With L'Etoile going full steam ahead, I asked him if he's had a relatively easy time of it so far. Sure enough, his crop has seen pests and disease, but nothing that he feels can't be managed in a safe and environmentally benign way.

Each year of experience represents a year of study. With knowledge and careful attention to soil fertility, L'Etoile says, "It looks like this is going to work out for us. We're starting to get it. UVM's been very helpful."

From that kind of feedback, Darby takes heart. "Most growers are still learning a lot," she says. "There is a lot to learn. It's a very immature industry but it's coming."

AUTUMN TREEHOUSE

The bright sunshine slants lower on the sky as the first calendar days of fall swing the northern hemisphere closer to the sun. Closer, yet cooler every day, as the hours of sunlight shrink with each dawn, providing just one element of the bittersweet emotion this season of transition always brings.

All the autumn traditions kick in: picking pumpkins, eating apples, raking leaves, and enjoying the recent harvest as it infuses fall brews with freshness and sustenance. Soon the season of Oktoberfest will be here with its assorted outdoor celebrations in area towns.

Apples start to snap with sweet juice after long cool nights in September. Area orchards look impossibly full this year. Turns out the local hop crop provided a bounty as well. Brimfield, Massachusetts is a little town made famous by the flea market held here twice a year. Now, a very small brewery named Tree House Brewing Company calls the town home. Open only one day a week, the forty gallons or so available at that time is always sold out before the scheduled 6 P.M. close.

A little website monitoring revealed this week's selections, and among them, a beer made with locally grown hops. Simply called Local Nugget, this ale got its name from hops grown less than ten minutes away at a Tree House customer's Warren home. A local, wet-hopped ale is not be passed up, especially only twenty minutes from my door.

This got my engine running. I didn't want to dally and chance missing out on local hops. Rising up the side of St. Clair Road, I know we've arrived when the narrow and empty street suddenly has cars parked on the side. Looking left, I spot a nondescript wooden sign and several people milling about a koi pond. Others relax on the deck chairs, tasting glasses in their hands. This is the place.

Inside the small red brewhouse, several customers stand by a bar stacked with 750-milliliter flip-top bottles. Three young ladies busily fill the bottles but kindly offer to pour Suzanne and me a couple flights of the three beers on tap. After placing our snifters on the wooden paddles in front of us, our bartender recommends that we work left to right. This fits with the standard tasting format: lighter to darker.

On the other hand, I want the local hops to be first on my parched tongue, so I start in the middle. I am not disappointed. Local Nugget is thick with lupulin resin like a room with a freshly installed Christmas tree. Normally used as a bittering agent, the Nugget in this double IPA does not hit the back of the palate with a lingering bite like many big hoppy beers will. When used as a flavoring and aroma ingredient, Nugget tends to be herbal, but here I am loving a floral scent on top of the plunge into an evergreen forest.

That dramatic difference, between what is normally expected from the variety and what is found in this glass, has a few possible causes. Used fresh, the flavors still contain the most volatile of oils that would otherwise dissipate. The dried version may be more intense, since the weight is reduced by 75 percent, but the density of aromas present in my glass are self-evident. Another factor that seems likely are differences in terrain between the typical western hop and this product from the hilly central New England town.

As we sip along, Suzanne gains permission to noodle around on one of several guitars in the room and Dean Rohan introduces himself as one of the proprietors. I comment on my appreciation of local hops. Rohan says when the hops arrived at the brewery, he opened the bag and could not believe the aromas. These hops, he says, "were the most gorgeous." This fleeting and tiny batch of native hopped beer is a great example of what locally grown ingredients can do. Nugget hops from Warren have characteristics unlike any Nugget I'd ever had, and far better. The reason it's better is no mystery at all—local is fresher.

Rohan doesn't linger as new customers continue to pour in, empty bottles in hand or in boxes. He is replaced at my side by a three-legged retriever with a red bandana who introduces himself by trying to stick his wet nose into my palm in an effort to swipe a peanut. Sad brown eyes make it clear my new friend doesn't mean any harm. Simple peanut craving, plus an overdeveloped sense of smell, leaves him at the mercy of his nose. In some ways, I can relate.

Snifters drained, I ask for another flight, but learn with a disapproving glance from the bartender that the rule is only one per customer. This being Massachusetts, the Commonwealth of the arcane liquor laws, I am not surprised. If I want more, and I do, I have to pay for a bottle. So I do.

As my order is added to the end of a long line, I step outside and take in the view to the southwest. From this hillside, I can see what I reckon is the little valley of Chicopee Brook and beyond that a ridge line in Palmer. In the foreground, perched in a copse of trees, the eponymous tree house looks fit for daily living. Meanwhile, Rohan and another Tree House employee have begun jamming with Suzanne, providing a rollicking show for those who patiently wait for their precious refills. Like any neighborhood brewery, this place offers something else with its beer: a chance to make friends quick. Finally, with a bottle of nuggety goodness in hand, we have to depart, and like everything else this time of year, our time at Tree House was naturally fleeting.

A short time later, it became clear that this little remote brewery needed to expand. Customers showed up in droves. Wait times for bottle fills grew into the four hour range as thirsty people came from near and far. Having tasted the local harvest, the Tree House brewery team decided to move to a farm in nearby Monson so they could both accommodate their numerous faithful and produce their own ingredients.

FOR THE LOVE OF BEER

It's that time of the spring when the sun feels warm, but the breeze carries colder air out from the shadows and skin gets little bumps from the chill. When a cloud cuts out the sun, we all tighten our shoulders in a reflexive effort to keep in our little dose of solar warmth.

Looking down along the neat rows punctuated by repurposed telephone poles on this south-facing hillside in southern Maine, I detect little green spikes, each with an inch long serrated leaf or two. Quickly, almost while you watch, these perky shoots will grab a line and climb like a craft beer sales graph, not stopping until they are all the way to the top, some twenty feet in the air. Next to me is someone who knows a few things about craft beer sales and the incredible popularity of hops. His name is Paul Allard and he works for Willamette Valley Hops in Oregon. He knows most of the brewers I've met, having sold them what they could not get locally, and indirectly, some of the local supply as well.

The hops we're inspecting now grow from rhizomes he sold. As we chat, I ask him what he thinks about the northeast industry's chances for success. The biggest obstacle, he confirms, is harvest preservation. He says turning hops into pellets is the best way of limiting the destabilizing effects of oxygen exposure. Hop pellet machines, like they have in the major growing regions, work in controlled environments, pressing the hops into dense little cylinders and then quickly freezing them. These machines cost multiple millions of dollars. Allard doesn't see the economy of scale working in favor of that kind of investment in the Northeast.

That doesn't worry his brother-in-laws, Doug and Jeff Therrien. This is their hop farm in Springvale, Maine, called Rock Island for the pile of stones in the middle of the field placed there by some long ago farmer who cleared this land.

The Therriens don't fret too much about preserving hops right now because everything they grow is used fresh. "The day we pick, we drive down to the brewery and it goes right in," Doug explains. The exception is their Nugget harvest, which goes into Peak Organic's Hop Noir, and is dried on homemade racks. The Centennial they grow goes into a beer that same day at Bunker Brewing, also in nearby Portland.

Most of what Rock Island grows is Cascade, and all of that goes to a third Portland brewery, Sebago. When the hops are ready, the farmers simply cut the bines and drive them over to the brewery where they are picked. "They had food and beer and it was a party," says Doug. The result is Local Harvest Ale made with 100 percent local ingredients.

The Therriens have saved me the last bottle. This beer, generically styled an "ale," is a one-of-a-kind original. Not a Brown Ale, but the malt is up front with a sweet touch of caramel and cashew. Not an IPA for certain, but after a few sips, the hops are revealed to be present in strength, exhibiting that wet hop ability to fold smoothly into the malt flavor profile. Nor does this beer want to copy any other well-known style that was developed in a faraway place. It's simply an expression of the regional terrain, impossible to recreate elsewhere, though good enough to make others want to try.

It can't happen, however, because New England brewers buy all of the local supply and will, for the foreseeable future, continue to keep it all to themselves. I sip slowly, not wanting the last vestige of this Rock Island hop crop to be gone before I wring every flavor molecule from it. The way various characteristics blend seamlessly into one body gives this beer a different profile than the sharply defined flavors dominating the craft market. But in a crowded field getting more crowed every day, a different direction can help a beer stand out.

Sebago likes their Rock Island Cascade so much, they want more. Recently, two more rows were planted. "We can't grow enough Cascade," Doug says. "They'll take all we can grow. The response has been unbelievable. It was supposed to be a fun little project. Now, we could grow as much as we want. It's a seven-acre field. We never thought it would be anything like this, just the amount of local support. We go into Sebago and we're treated like royalty." The owner himself gets behind the bar and pours beers for his hop farmers. Yet, to these guys, it's the brewers who are the rock stars. And Doug and Jeff like rubbing elbows as much as any fan would. "It's the best," Doug says. "When Chresten from Bunker came down to the field and Jon from Peak and Kai from Sebago, it feels like we've become part of the brewing culture."

This inclusion has bred loyalty in the Therrien brothers. They drink only Maine-made beers. I can relate. Having lived in Maine until 2004, I never found the need for anything beyond Gritty McDuff's, Federal Jack's, Geary's, Casco Bay, and Sea Dog. Now there are a great many more Maine brewers to choose from. Jeff says, "Nothing wrong with other places, but, you know, we like to support the local guys."

"And they support us," Doug adds.

At about a quarter-acre, this little plot of ground behind their parents' house keeps Doug and Jeff busy on weekends mulching, pruning, watering, and so forth. During the week they run a retail and wholesale tire business with their father. As much as that business thrives and as much as they enjoy solving problems to keep it going smoothly, beer has captured their hearts. Not just any beer, either, but hop forward beers have made them devotees. "We love IPAs," Doug says. "The first time I tried one, it was just . . . this is good." A fascination with hops followed and a few years ago they planted some rhizomes.

Today, says Jeff, they've put $15,000 into constructing permanent trellises and buying hundreds of plants. Still, they've tried to save money at every turn. "Farming on a shoestring," Jeff says. "That's what this is."

One of the more frugal pieces of equipment is the harvesting platform that they built themselves. A commercial-sized truck, with their tire company's name on the doors, has been retrofitted with railings and metal grates for a stage, raised up on poles welded to the bed of the truck. They use it to cut the bines down at harvest time and secure the lines in the spring. "We call it the Tuna Tower," Doug says. "For us, that was the easy part. We've always had to fabricate things for the business. We had this old truck and some scrap metal."

For all the effort and money they've spent, I have to ask if they expect a pretty good return. Jeff puts his arms out to the side, palms up. "We haven't really made anything yet," he says. "We do all this for the love of beer."

Knowing they are confirmed hop heads, I thought they might like to try a couple of brewers also featured in these pages. Wormtown's Hopulance and Brewmaster Jack's Imperial IPA made the trip north with me and I pull them from their icy storage in my little briefcase cooler.

As we pass the bottles around, both these beers catch me by surprise. The Hopulance label describes the contents as having 120 IBUs. Truthfully, that bit of information has me a little intimidated. With 30 percent more IBUs than Wormtown's Be Hoppy, a beer that overpowers my taste buds and leaves me wondering if I enjoyed it or it enjoyed me, I expect Hopulance to burst in my mouth with bitterness and thick resin. I say all that with the caveat that, while I do list many IPAs among my favorite beers, unlike many people I know, I don't like every IPA I've ever tried. Hoppier is not always better in my book.

But the Therriens are intrigued. "I've never had a beer with 120," Doug says, filling his mouth almost before he finishes his thought. "Wow, that's really good." Jeff has the same reaction. My turn, and to my pleasant surprise, this beer bursts not with resiny bitterness, but with tropical fruit, aromas right out of an orchard in bloom, and an overall smooth malt feel. Wow, that is really good. False expectations won't keep me from the happiness of yet another beer to love.

Next, I crack open the Brewmaster's creation made with 100 percent regionally grown grain malted at Valley Malt. Labeled an Imperial IPA, this beer is also not what I expect. The malt is in the forefront here, as is often the case with the local stuff. Yes, there is a matching bitterness and some hop notes in the flavor, but again, I enjoy it more than I expect. To me, it tastes closer to a strong stock ale than a punchy IPA. And the hop heads with me seem to prefer the extremely aromatic Hopulance. That's okay. I can get more when I get home. Meanwhile, Brewmaster Jack is just as delicious in its own way. With these beers smoothing the way, we are fast becoming friends. As we say our good-byes, I already look forward to coming back for next year's Local Harvest Ale. Good beer means good times.

WILD CARD

My homebrew buddy, John, led me to a thin screen of trees before the woods thickened into impenetrable jumbles of brush and vine. "There's one," he said, stepping through knee-high spring growth of dozens of kinds of forest vegetation. Then I saw one. A string of green with purple highlights slightly curved at the top, as if bending its head in search of something to hold onto. The little stalk bobbed slightly in the still air, as if feeling its surroundings. Then I saw more. Some were already climbing up the sides of trees, long thin green lines reaching branches overhead. I scanned the area around me and suddenly could see them everywhere. Hops!

Without another word, we began sinking our spades into the forest floor on the edge of his woodsy, garden-centric North Brookfield, Massachusetts home. John would transplant his from the tree line to the side of the barn where they are now dressed in every available ounce of sunlight. I took mine home and planted them along any vertical object I could find, including the corner of the garage, the swing set frame and the chicken coop.

After the first harvest, we brewed several batches with them and found the flavor a little like chamomile with sageish undertones and flashes of apple or pear and very delicious. Used fresh, they gave off the sweet smell of fresh cut meadow with a honeydew fruitiness. It reminds me of Fuggles, the first hop I ever grew. But where did these mystery hops come from? Were they planted there by some long ago farmer or were they native hops, growing wild? So I called the hop expert on my list, UVM's Heather Darby. She says they are likely survivors of a defunct local hop farm. She guesses that it could be a variety called Cluster that was grown in this region in the 1800s, but without an expensive DNA test there is no way to positively identify it. Even with the test, she says, not all varieties are in the database. She recommends making a tea from a few cones to see what it tastes like.

Yet, it could be a native species, I think. Some sources do point to the existence of a North American native hop that grew in the Northeast when the colonists arrived. According to the USDA hop breeding program, native populations are generally free of diseases common to commercial hops. As a result, the USDA has focused on crossing native genes with commercial plants in hopes of developing the best flavor and hardiness of each.

Jon Cadoux of Peak Organic once ran into a mystery hop from the wild. "We found a wild strain in Maine two years ago and sent it in to a lab." Based on the components in the hop cone, Cadoux says, "It's similar, in overall content, to Cascade." The discovery made an impression. He could see in these wild plants that hops not only can grow in this region, but sometimes they do so without any help at all. The ones he found were growing in a bog. "Unbelievable," he says. "It's a complete mystery."

Pedersen Farm in Seneca Castle has been seizing on the native hop as a primary crop. They focus on a landrace variety named New York that they say was grown commercially in the 1800s. What else is there to learn from these woods and backyard gardens? Will the natural selection of 150 years provide us a volunteer hop adapted to the Northeast, ready to be the next big thing? Wild hop sightings are many. The hunt is on.

BREWYARDS

The air is as warm as laundry fresh from the dryer. That comfortable feeling of being cradled by the season embraces us as we head for a few days on Cape Elizabeth, courtesy of family and friends. Two hours into the drive, our bellies rumble. Fortunately for us, Portsmouth, New Hampshire, a city well stocked with good eats, lay at the end of the next exit ramp. What we need is a solid burger joint. And a great beer. I've done my homework. I know where to find both—Lexie's Joint on Islington Avenue where they pour Throwback Brewery and go all out for a tasty burger in the form of beef, chicken or bean patties.

Suzanne and I opened with Throwback's Bohemian pilsner called Love Me Long Time. Crisp and delicious, this is one fine example of the genre, but made with a decidedly non-traditional ingredient: Willamette hops grown in the Northeast. This variety is said to provide earthy and spicy characteristics. Here, it is just right in complementing the noble Perle. There is a definite tang, a tease of subtleties that dances over the biscuity malt . . . but wait a minute, it's gone. That was fast. The only way to love this one a long time is by the case.

Oh well, here comes our Dippity Do American Brown Ale. This is the kind of brown that makes you wonder what black is. Dark and mysterious on the blazing bright day, I let my nose hover over the off-white half-inch of foam sizzling in the glass. Mild? Yes, and it has no stouty coffee or chocolate either. Interesting. The mystery deepens. I must investigate.

The first mouthful is again a surprise. Roasty, but fading. And after that, a hint of molasses dissolves into the final clean finish of hops. Medium body belies the dense appearance and begs for another mouthful. I oblige. This beer, more pleasing with each ensuing taste, is made with wheat malt grown at Brookford Farm in Rollinsford, New Hampshire, two-row barley malt and Munich malt grown at Qualey Farms, Inc. in Benedicta, Maine, and Willamette hops grown at Foothill Hops Farm in Madison County, New York. In addition to being local, these ingredients were grown organically.

Meanwhile, the kids are into milkshakes and hand-cut French fries. The burgers vanish and we must move on. Lexie's is quick, but makes an impression—thanks to the basics done with care and Throwback Brewery providing beer that seems made to drink with burgers and fries—an experience both filling and fulfilling to know that local farmers get our business.

FARM BREW

For more and more brewers, the use of local ingredients has become a fully involved process. To several brewers, this means not only buying locally raised ingredients, but growing them as well. In North Hampton, New Hampshire, less than four miles from the sea, Throwback Brewery recently purchased a farm at auction. Not only do they now have a new home for their brewery with room for expansion, but they will be teaming up with a local farmer to grow ingredients for their beer on site, including an acre of hops. Furthermore, this land had been farmed since the 1700s. On the auction block, the highest bidder could have been someone who would put an end to all that rural character. This region has quite a tradition of converting farmland to other uses. More and more, that trend is shifting back.

In 1862, the owners of this property, known as Hobbs Farm, built a Victorian grand mansion and barn. A dairy farm operated there from the 1930s to the mid-1950s. From that point, sheep were raised until about 1990. Most recently, the estate passed into the hands of a grandson who made the decision to sell. This coastal, expensive property appeared doomed to become office space, retail or more single-family homes built on speculation.

Not so fast. Out of all the possible outcomes, a nearby brewery stepped in and saved the farm. How many industries would have found it worthwhile to pony up almost a million dollars for thirty acres of prime real estate with frontage on three roads and kept its use as a farm? These properties typically go to a developer or corporation. Yet, in this case, a craft brewer saw the value in agriculture. To be fair, Throwback Brewery is not your average beer maker. They've established their business practices on the principle of local first.

When it came to their initial equipment purchases, they doubled down on sustainability. Rather than having a brand new system made and shipped to them, they found used tanks nearby and had a local welder assemble what they fondly call their Frankenbrewery. The result is not the prettiest of systems, but contributes in satisfying ways to their mission.

"We try to source everything within 200 miles," says cofounder Nicole Carrier. "We're sixty to seventy percent there. Having local malts has been great." She refers to Throwback's membership in Valley Malt's Brewer Supported Agriculture program. Valley Malt is, of course, another beer industry business that got into farming. Genetics may be at play here, since Carrier turns out to be Andrea Stanley's cousin. But for Throwback, buying local malt is more than just keeping it in the family.

Before venturing into professional brewing in 2010, Carrier and her partner, Annette Lee, already shared an appreciation for fresh and local food as well as brewing their own beer. "Personally, both Annette and myself get most of our food from farmers' markets," Carrier says. Buying local food has several positive outcomes, she explains. "It's helping the community and the environment and as gas goes up, it may one day be cheaper."

When they went into business together, it was natural to extend their farm support to the way they run the brewery. "We were living our life like this," Carrier says. "And since a new business is like a baby, why feed the baby something different? This is how we live our personal lives. So to do business this way made sense."

For Lee, who already had a full career as an environmental engineer, the brewing process has always held a special appeal. Over the years, she sunk herself deeper into the technical aspects, taking classes at the Siebel Institute of Technology in Chicago and landing an internship at Smuttynose Brewing Company in Portsmouth, New Hampshire. Soon, she designed the brewing system and launched a new career. "She was insane enough to quit her job," Carrier says, proudly. "It's been fun."

One beneficial result has been more than that. "The sense of community," Carrier says, "has been very powerful and rewarding." From farmers who live in the area to beer fans who do, too, "There is a community that comes together in the tap room. I never thought we'd be connecting people together like this." Beer does that. Native beer does it better.

The partners have a division of labor that allows them each to focus on their strengths. Lee, the former engineer, is the brewer. Carrier says, "I'm business and marketing and the food side. I provide the artistry and think up recipes for our food-oriented beers." One look at the Throwback beer list and I see how important food is to their creative process. Ingredients include chocolate, peanut butter, mushrooms, rhubarb, jalapenos, and plenty of others foods and herbs. The site also sports numerous food pairing suggestions as well as recipes. At the farm, they will be able to provide a lot of these ingredients and more for themselves. Carrier is already thinking about the rhubarb, coriander, raspberries, and grains they will grow. The idea, she says, is to produce "estate" beer.

With plans to move into a large barn on their new property, Throwback is no longer a two-person show. They've hired three employees so far, including a pair of brewing assistants and now find themselves brewing three to four times per week, up from once per week after they opened. In her mind's eye, Carrier sees solar panels. "The barn would be perfect," she says. Wind power may come first. "We have a windmill in our logo," she explains. A stone's throw from the Atlantic, she points out, "We have a pretty windy field, too."

While the unusual beer ingredients help set Throwback apart, Carrier knows that without grain, their local mission would fail. She speaks with deep appreciation in her voice, pointing to one farmer in particular. "Luke Mahoney at Brookford Farm grows amazing red and white winter wheat for many of our beers." In part because their wheat comes from only a few miles away, many of their beers are designed to use it.

This is an opposite approach from what most brewers take. Instead of thinking about what to make, which is largely based on what is popular and then ordering the ingredients to match the style, Throwback thinks about what is close by, then designs a beer to match what is available—a perspective they no doubt sharpened living off the seasonal variety of a farmers' market.

As Heather Darby points out, the future of local ingredients lies in making beer to accentuate the flavors from this terrain. Simply put, with farmers adding more acres and Valley Malt doing all they can, it's now up to the brewers to bring out the terroir of their region, not by copying West Coast or European styles, but by highlighting the local flavors. Throwback has taken up the challenge and the results have been very well received.

In addition to malted grains, Throwback uses local oats. They also get many of their hops from northern Maine and New York, though this is not a brewery that has hopped on the bandwagon, so to speak. While hops seem to be the only thing on some brewers' minds, Throwback lets other ingredients shine as well, a practice illustrated by their beer list.

Maple-Kissed Wheat Porter, for example, uses local maple and grain. This beer is on the dark side and the wheat provides a creamy texture. The syrup adds notes of sweetness, of course, but also that unmistakable flavor of an authentic New England breakfast that is uniquely maple. A roasted grain addition offers another rustic dimension. For those of us who have been captivated by smoked foods, the Campfire Ale has what we need. The Throwback crew smokes the malt themselves atop a barbecue grill. Yes it's rudimentary, but we're talking Campfire here. And it works. The applewood embers impart that mouth watering cookout aroma and with a spicy barbecue, there is no better brew. Or, for the liquid dieters, a growler of Campfire might go nicely with a Spicy Bohemian, which is the Pilsner infused with roasted jalapeno peppers. Produced from mid-summer through the first frost, when the peppers wilt in the chill, the organic grain comes from Lake Shore Farms in St. David, Maine via Valley Malt.

Even Throwback's traditional styles have a distinct, New England twist. Hog Happy Hefeweizen, a traditional wheat beer that is not very hoppy and bitter, uses a special kind of yeast to bring out flavors of banana and clove. The wheat in Throwback's version is locally sourced and possesses characteristics not found in Bavarian wheat. The beer's name comes from the practice of sending the spent grains out to feed livestock, including a few joyful pigs. As the website states, "Drink a beer, feed a pig."

Oma's Tribute is a German style called Schwarzbier because of the characteristic dark brown color. Smooth and roasty, this is another beer where the hops keep a low profile. Ingredients include organic and local Pilsen malt. Hopstruck fits the bill for the throngs of hop lovers. A red IPA with that signature citrus aroma and a bracing bitter finish. Two-row barley provides the base malt along with Crystal and Munich and was grown organically at Qualey Farms. The organic Willamette hops grew at Foothill Hops Farm.

If they are going to meet their goal of 100 percent local beer, Carrier knows they will need to overcome quite a few challenges. Local prices will be higher, at least in the beginning. The climate cannot provide the full spectrum of ingredients found on the global market, but meeting challenges and overcoming them with creativity, determination, and cooperation with other like-minded people is what makes life worthwhile. Just because no else is doing it, doesn't mean it can't be done. Throwback is old fashioned like that.

Again from the website, "Our team is inherently optimistic." A common thread in these pages is people believing in themselves enough to forge a new road instead of following the crowd. And it's not blind faith. Throwback has a basis for their business plan. Carrier feels that the expanding buy local movement will lead to their door. People who want to know where their lettuce is grown will also find it appealing to know their beer grew at a nearby farm. "We made up a word," she says. "Beeroir." Where terroir is applied to wine and cheese, something about it doesn't work when discussing beer.

Carrier is blunt. "Terroir is a somewhat pretentious word," she says. With wine, each producing region confers distinct attributes and wine makers are required to cite the region where the grapes were sourced. The place is essential to their identity. "With wine it's okay to have terroir," she says, "but with beer, a lot of people expect beer to taste the same all the time." Local ingredients come with an inherent inconsistency. Take, for example, the Jalapeños. "Depending on the time of the season, they could be spicy or mild. You always get that pepper aroma, but in a hot season, the peppers get hot," Carrier explains.

The popularity of the Spicy Bohemian may serve to demonstrate that consistency of flavor is not the be-all, end-all many brewers think. Wine drinkers are prepared to have a favorite vintage of the exact same variety because they think of their drink as an agricultural product susceptible to seasonal variances. Couldn't beer drinkers develop the same level of awareness? Turns out, Carrier has learned from them.

"Our customers like variety," she says. Throwback could tweak their recipe and process to try to get each batch the same, but they like experiencing the progression of the season in the results.

The *beeroir* of New England has not yet earned any sort of label. Maybe one day, sooner than you think, beer from here and only from here will be called New Englander.

MOM AND POP'S HOPS

Framingham, Massachusetts is definitely not a farming community. But at Jack's Abby Brewing, one beer is made with their very own hops. For starters, they have a row of hops improbably growing in a sliver of unpaved ground between the road and the parking lot. These are Cascade bines and they were transplanted from the family farm where Jack Hendler's parents grow luscious and vibrant cones for Mom and Pop's Wet Hop Lager, one of the most memorably delicious concoctions I've ever tried.

Every year, when the crop ripens, it's time for the Hendler family to gather around and start picking, a tradition with roots laid down in 2005. Jack tells it like this: "My mom visited my aunt in Washington state and saw hops growing. It was a novelty. She brought home one rhizome." Today, he says, "My parents grow a lot of hops at their farm in Vermont."

Primarily they grow Cascade. Hendler calls it "our dominant variety. It's the most disease and insect resistant." They also grow Centennial and Nuggett, strains that have caught on in the region. Last year they harvested 200 pounds and put them all fresh into the annual wet hop batch. It wasn't quite enough, so they supplemented with 100 pounds or so from Four Star Farms. With that, they turned out forty barrels plus thirty to forty kegs. "There's only a small window for wet hopping," Hendler says, almost apologetically. "There's only so much you can brew."

Good fortune and a timely trip to Mass Liquors on Chandler Street in Worcester, put a four-pack of the Mom and Pop's in my hand. Wet hops are often described as floral, but that makes me think of sticking my nose in a bouquet. These wet hops are like a spring meadow after fresh rain—like honeysuckle faint on a breeze, but also juicy with fruit flavors that bounce from pear to melon to lime in ways that maddeningly disappear almost before they can be perceived. The nuances in every taste keep me tipping my glass.

Hendler explains why he uses his own hops fresh rather than dried. "Hops have a short shelf-life if they're not processed properly. Honestly, the quality of dried local hops is not up to what we can get from out west. We've tried local hops that have been dried and packaged and found the volatile compounds that give hops its flavor are far superior from the northwest." He says that spells death in a marketplace where hop heads rule and IPA is king. "You can't compete with subpar hops."

Hendler's perspective points again to the missing piece in the immature northeast hop growing industry: equipment. Hendler cites other factors that also stand in the way of local hops. "I've seen the hops out there," he says, meaning the northwest. "They're bigger, taller, fatter cones. Out here, we try to do it organic, but it's prone to insects and disease. It's not easy to grow."

For now, he takes solace in his annual wet hopping. "It's counterintuitive," he says. "Wet hops are less aromatic. The majority of it is water. Drying concentrates flavors. Wet are more mellow, more of the terroir. You get the flavor of the farm. That's what we like. It's truly unique." Beyond the hop content, the grain bill is locally sourced. For Mom and Pop's, Jack's Abby wanted to go all out. They called up Valley Malt, but they also added unmalted wheat, spelt, and triticale for a 100 percent local beer.

As much as Hendler likes working with local products, he says each harvest comes with a level of uncertainty. "With local ingredients, you get what you get." He points out that local malt has been far more reliable than hops. "We put local grain in all of our beers. The problem there is supply. Valley Malt is selling everything they make. We've just put in an order for 8,000 pounds." That malt will go into a collaborative brew by Jack's and Lawson's Finest of Vermont, but it was no sure thing. "Valley Malt had to work it into their schedule," he says.

As for brewing with Lawson, Hendler explains how naturally the connection was made. "Sean has family nearby and he just stopped in. We got to talking and we said why don't we do a beer together?" Since they both have a Vermont connection, this beer will feature a lot of Green Mountain character, thanks to an infusion of maple syrup. "We were going to make it with maple from my parents' farm," he says, "but the sugar shack wasn't ready so, it'll be Vermont syrup from a nearby farm and 100 percent local malt." Make that smoked malt. According to Hendler, Lawson is harvesting maple wood for this special use. The grain bill will also include brown malt and caramunich.

Hendler feeds his brewing system a steady diet of local rye malt. "Rye has a unique flavor," he says. "Sometimes it works. Sometimes it doesn't. And it's difficult to work with. The grain has no hull, so it gummies up. There's more protein than in barley. It makes it very difficult." Liquid extraction is the name of the game, but with rye, the liquid can remain sealed in a pasty mass, leaving a brewer with a mess. To facilitate the use of what's locally available, Hendler employs a work-around. "We add rice hulls to help separate liquid from solid."

When he compares local malt to the mainstream supply, he sees some differences. "The quality is there. The difference is mostly in the mill. Local grains vary in size. They're not as uniform to work with and they tend to be smaller kernels than the ones from the Midwest. That's probably due to farming methods, Hendler reasons. "I think the small farms don't use quite as much fertilizer. They're more likely to be organic. That might be part of it. And with the Midwest barley, they separate it by size. The bigger ones go to brewers and smaller ones go to feed."

Smoke & Dagger (barley) and Hoponius Union (spelt)—Hendler explains that when unmalted grains are added to the kettle, the enzymes in the malted grains work to unlock the sugars in the unmalted, as well. The beer derives certain characteristics from using unmalted grains that cannot be found otherwise. For instance, unmalted grain contains more protein which provides for a fuller body in the brew. In all, Jack's Abby uses 5 percent local grain which amounts to about 25,000 pounds. Hendler says, "That's only going to grow as we grow."

Three other notable farm breweries include 5 Mile Ales of Massachusetts, Thomas Hooker Brewing of Connecticut, and The Prodigal Brewery of New Hampshire. To varying degrees, these brewers devote themselves to bringing in their own harvests.

5 Mile is a brand put out by Rob Martin of Ipswich Ale Brewery with the premise being that a majority of the ingredients come from within five miles of Ipswich. Martin does that by leasing land on existing farms to grow his own grains. He also owns his own combine harvester to get the crop in.

The same arrangement works with hops. One farm where Martin has formed a partnership has been owned by the Marini family since 1928. According to Michael Marini, Martin gets rye from their fields. "Rob harvested it and continued the process along," he says. "Also I have leased him the land for his hops, buts his team has taken on the growing and harvest."

This being a new arrangement, Marini says, "There is not much impact for our farm because the acreage grown is very small and it's kind of in the trial stages. But I think the local connection is really great and is a win-win for both of us. Hops is a perennial crop and open land is such a limited resource that the numbers would really have to work to justify the land usage."

TAVERNS OF THE LAND

Suzanne and I are heading to Cambridge, Massachusetts for good grub and suds. What a surprise. As we are not very hip and our phones couldn't be called smart and our car is not fitted with global positioning systems via satellite transmission, we miss the turn and are no longer in Cambridge at all. In fact, across the bridge over the Charles River we find a turnaround near Boston's North End. Pizza, anyone?

Not today. This frigid, bitterly windy "spring" day is all about beer. Our destination is Kendall Square. We decide to park in the first garage we see in Cambridge and follow our noses. Maybe the wind has disguised the direction of the scent of chorizo and fresh brews because we have to ask a man on the street where to go. As soon as the words leave my mouth I brace for a wiseacre remark, but our impromptu guide points us just around the corner and then says, "Enjoy yourselves, folks." Obviously a beer drinker.

Cambridge is famously known for Harvard University, which is in the other end of town, and the Massachusetts Institute of Technology, which is in the neighborhood we are walking through. Following the instructions of our happy Cambridge helper takes us into a wind tunnel between several new sterile looking buildings with stainless steel and glass themes and signs that bear names like Cambridge Laboratories and BioGen. Brrr. The temperature on this bright and sunny day seems to plummet.

As we pass through the pedestrian mall to the street on the other side, I see signs of life. A pub. People. A rent-a-bike rack. Traffic. But this is where the brewery is supposed to be and I don't see that until I turn all the way around. Behind me, almost obscured by one of the newer buildings, is an arched sign that says Cambridge Brewing Company. At last, I think to myself, now that I've found you, I'll never let you go.

The front room at CBC heads off to the right of the entrance in a pair of long rows parallel to the bar. Dark wood and windows onto the patio characterize the setting. Suzanne has free entertainment in the form of a crew working to install the patio awning. Most of time we're there, many of cigarettes are smoked, heads scratched and little progress made. This just makes Suzanne feel as jolly as a leprechaun. The beer doesn't hurt.

My first choice is called Local Notion. Made with Valley Malt, Local Notion is an American Pale Ale with enough hops to complement the sweet honey aroma and fresh grain flavor of the barley. Medium to full-bodied, I get complex flavors that range from orange zest to English muffin.

For her first beer, Suzanne opts for a cask-conditioned ale, which is currently a dry hopped porter. I, too, am always tempted by casked beers. They are more natural tasting, with lighter carbonation and fresher flavor than kegged beer. Plus they harken back to a time before industrialization when the main source of power for getting beer into a cup was gravity, which is about as sustainable a power source as there could be. Modern kegs are usually force-carbonated with pressurized CO_2 gas tanks, then moved from the kegs to the tap using the same energy intensive power source. The bubbles are fatter than natural yeast carbonation.

The Local Notion comes in a tulip-shaped glass and the porter is served in a traditional pint. CBC sells larger sizes, as well. The pitcher of beer is a serving many bars offer, but I never saw a beer tower until I walked through these doors. That's right. Pillars of pale ale. Monuments to malt juice. Skyscrapers of kolsch. The party of four next to us has been draining what looks like an overgrown test tube of golden yellow ale, their faces spread out in smiles. I may ask if they need any help. If we didn't have to drive, or we had several friends along . . . .

For now, we order buffalo chicken, mainly because whenever I see it on the menu my mouth starts to water and I can't think of anything else. Here, the chicken is at least raised naturally and humanely instead of in overcrowded cages, beakless, featherless and fed antibiotics and GMO corn. And these are, in the breadth of my experience on this subject, the best dang boneless wings I've ever had. The Buffalo chicken paired beautifully with the Local Notion.

Next comes the Smokin' in the Valley Amber Ale. Dark brown and pungent with cherry wood fire, it further enhances the last few spicy bites of chicken. With this one, CBC uses three flavors from Valley Malt. The amber malt provides an underlying toasty character while the chocolate rye malt provides a layer of baker's chocolate along with the white pepper bite of rye in the background. Cherry wood smoked two-row barley malt infuses the beer with the pleasing aroma of a hardwood fire as well as distinct components of dried cherries, which made the wings taste like they'd been cooked on a wood fire.

Before I am half finished with this beer, chorizo and clams with arugula arrives, along with smoked trout and marinated red onions on a bed of mixed greens. The clams are from Wellfleet, Massachusetts according to the menu and the dish is a riff on a traditional Portuguese American combo commonly found in the southeastern part of the state. Suzanne, as a native to that area and of partial Portuguese descent, says "That was the best clam I ever had."

The meaty morsels glisten with the red juices of the spicy sausage and I dive in. Toothsome, briny, sweet and peppery, the flavors send me to Horseneck Beach and I can almost feel a warm sea breeze filling my head with oxygen and minerals. With the traditional dish, the red sausage would more likely be linguica and the greens would be kale instead of arugula, but this combination proves even better.

New England shellfish is considered one of the few remaining sustainable seafoods. If it weren't, it wouldn't be on the menu at CBC. Here, only seafood from stable populations with verifiable origins will be served. Not only that, but in the same way CBC buys its malt straight from the source via the BSA program, they also prefer to buy directly from the fishermen themselves.

According to the CBC founder Phil Bannatyne, "Independent fishermen are trying to find ways to distribute directly to restaurants. That way they can get their price." He says many of those fishermen call Scituate their home port. So the flavors of that southeastern port come in on the tide of hardshell clams common to those shores.

We ate everything but the shells, but in most cases, plates return to the kitchen of any restaurant with at least some food left. Most places promptly deposit these leftovers into plastic trash bags bound for a garbage truck. Where the truck takes it depends. Only a fraction of Massachusetts' waste goes to area landfills due to the fact that most landfills in the state have already been filled. Often times the trash is delivered to a railroad car and takes a ride to places like western Pennsylvania where it can be buried, or other places that burn trash for electricity and emit toxic chemicals and deadly particulates into the atmosphere.

On the other hand, the food waste can be very useful. For example, for many years Portsmouth Brewery has taken the time to scrape food from plates into barrels reserved for a local farmer. This farmer happily comes to remove several barrels of the stuff almost every day to feed his pigs.

Bannatyne likes to feed the farm animals, too. That's where his spent brewing grains end up. As for CBC's food scraps, those become compost thanks to an outfit called Save that Stuff that makes regular curbside pick-ups and takes it to their North Shore composting facility where it's turned into what gardeners call "black gold."

"We pay for it, but there really isn't any trash coming out of this company other than some nasty plastic bags. Ninety percent of the restaurant waste is recycled or composted." This separation of compostables from recyclables not only costs more than just throwing it away, but takes more effort. They have to care. Bannatyne says, "We choose to recycle everything possible."

Those thought patterns had their roots in the very beginning when CBC opened its doors in 1989 with a plan to follow a passion. At first, the ability to do things in a sustainable way was quite limited. First, the concept of a brewpub had to be tested. CBC was one of the first one hundred in the nation and most of those were on the West Coast. Still, Bannatyne says, every time there is a decision to make, "We've always tried to do the right thing, the smart thing."

Twenty-four years later, smart choices are available in almost every component of the brewpub business. When did things change? Bannatyne thinks for a moment, then replies, "I would say in 2001, 2002, there was a consciousness elevation." People began to take the environment more seriously and realized their personal choices make a difference. "Doing the right thing became more obviously doing the most sustainable practices."

Then, looking at his own operations and the volume of material that comes through, Bannatyne realized CBC could do something big. "When you seat 3,000 people every week," he says, "you have an opportunity with that waste to make an impact. Being in Cambridge has been advantageous because we have a critical mass for the composting service." CBC provides eighty gallons per week to the pile.

Not only does the city of Cambridge have the population density that makes the numbers work for a compost hauler, but they have the mindset, too. As Bannatyne says, "Cambridge is a pretty forward-thinking community." In recent years, these elements have combined to create a business climate where CBC can fulfill its mission. After all, only a few years ago, there was no composting pick-up and there was no local malt. Times are changing, and CBC is helping to make that change.

Other ways they've been able to manifest this sustainable vision includes earth-friendly cleaning products and electricity-saving LED lights. "We use a lot of electricity," Bannatyne admits, explaining that it's "mostly for refrigeration." Still, he's found a way to make that power come from renewable energy. At the end of 2013, CBC contracted to receive 100 percent wind energy. And yes, it costs them more. "We pay a premium, but it's not prohibitive," says Bannatyne.

Another factor in the sustainability equation is how far the supplies travel. At CBC, decisions favor local sources whenever possible, even when it means leaving rock bottom prices half way across the world. For Bannatyne, the full cost of a product includes what happens to the environment, to the people, and to the future security of those vital supply lines. And they are not through at CBC. "We look around all the time for ways to be more sustainable."

He says the menu is a good reflection of how the local, ecologically conscious suppliers are stepping in. "We're seeing more and more small farms," he says. "The local food supply is expanding. In summer, almost all the produce is local to New England. We still get the big trucks. In the winter they bring lettuce, and French fries are year-round. We get #10 cans of ketchup." Yet, even after the growing season ends, Bannatyne finds that he can still get local vegetables. "One guy comes around once a week with parsnips and carrots. We get local when we can. We all think about ways to do more all the time."

Buying local is one thing, but making vittles that please their customer base involves a lot of creativity. "Local foods have terroir," Bannatyne says. As with beer, recipes that accentuate the ingredients in hand make it all work. Barley from New England is not generic barley and shouldn't be thought of as interchangeable. The same goes for tomatoes from western Massachusetts versus tomatoes from Florida. Same species, different animal.

Whenever local ingredients appear in their beers, CBC lets their customers know. "Everybody is excited about that," he says. "People are aware of the environmental damage done by long distance supplies. Customers want to do the right thing. We want to give them that chance."

All this has been a learning process for trailblazers like CBC. While most of their malt still comes from the Midwest, the fact that they can get regular shipments from Valley Malt has been a pleasant surprise. "I never thought when we started that I would be using Massachusetts-grown and malted barley," Bannatyne says. "I didn't anticipate that anyone could do that. But it started. It started to happen. They're visionaries. But as a percentage right now, we still use less than five. I do see that changing as Valley Malt expands. There is a market for it. It's a work in progress. We will continue to do whatever we can to support them. And a brewing supply industry is starting to develop locally. They're growing more acres all the time."

Their BSA membership has CBC waxing eloquent on their website. "We're always excited to work with their malts, as they close the gap between locally brewed beer and beer that is truly local. As brewers, we believe that beer can express terroir in much the same way as wine, provided that truly local ingredients are available." And now they are.

CBC grows a few hops on their patio, which adds a touch of green to the city square in spring. "These are really ornamental," Bannatyne says, "but we use them as a late addition in the boil." Whenever adjunct-type ingredients are needed, CBC scouts the native terrain for those, too. Heather comes from Westport and sugar pumpkins from Athol.

As we prepare to pay our check, Suzanne sips the last of her Spring Training IPA and asks for one to go . . . in a growler, that is. Made with Valley Malt pale and wheat malts, this hazy, fresh tasting IPA has flowers and spring breezes, and a laid back bitter finish. Now we must hurry home, so I can crack it open.

POWER TO THE PEOPLE'S

A raw day before Christmas finds us walking briskly the wrong way down Main Street in Greenfield, Massachusetts. The street shines with the kind of cold mist that gets under winter coats and into shoes, but I don't care. I'm with Suzanne and we are in this old mill town intent on patronizing the lively Main Street economy, after our first stop, that is. If we can find it. On the ride up our appetites ripened to the point of lip smacking. I need to stress that The People's Pint Brewery is easy to find. It's in downtown Greenfield—a very small town. Nothing is hard to find, but sometimes getting lost is a great way to get to know a place.

We turn around and walk back, peering down the side streets that are also filled with local businesses. No chains here. These are independent ventures competing daily with the fast food box store strip of pavement and cinder blocks out on the bypass. A slice of what was always best in small town America is still alive here and looking mighty good to these globalized eyes.

Okay, we have to ask for help. Hunger has rendered us helpless. Our kind stranger on the street points us back to where we've parked. Apparently, we walked right by it in our eagerness. Back at the car, we look left and a few doors down we can see a sign that makes our hearts sing—The People's Pint. My friend, it's been too long.

The inside seems exactly as I'd left it. Simplicity reigns. Wooden booths along the wall match the bar. All of it well kept, but careworn. This weekday afternoon, there are several empty seats. All of my past visits have been on crowded evenings. As we slide into a booth opposite each other, I have the sensation that the walls are quietly echoing all the cheerful clamor of the masses that have passed this way.

It takes a minute, but I recall there was never a television. Looking around, I am glad to find that is still the case. Essentially, there is not much to look at but each other. How could I mind that? But I know that this lack of distraction is no accident. The Pint was founded for the people, after all. There is no pressure to buy the fancy drinks or desserts displayed in full color on table tents in restaurants all over the world. Here, table tents and other glossy marketing clutter do not exist. The nondescript menu comes with a smiling waitress who does not go out of her way to fake being happy to see us. No, she's clearly being herself without an ounce of pretension and I, for one, am very grateful and even more at ease. I feel the complexities of the outside world, all the social conventions, the barrage of electronic images, the rat race itself—all of it—fading into the distance. I may never leave.

As if that weren't enough, The Pint happens to make really fine beers. As BSA members, they regularly offer flavors made with local ingredients. Naturally, this part I researched in advance. Star of the Valley is currently on tap, made with Valley Malt and Four Star Farms hops. Asking the waitress to describe the beer results in her wisely bringing me a sample. After all, taste is in the buds of the beholder.

A deep reddish brown, translucent and clear with a soft bed of light tan foam, this little glass will clearly not be enough. I sniff. Sweet, malty, nutty, and a hint at an herbal, almost marjoram aroma of hops. I sip. Nothing surprising. Just a fine, easy drinking beer. Exactly what I was hoping for. Naturally, I order a full glass which comes in the Valley Malt snifter.

Meanwhile, satisfied with a sip of mine, Suzanne wants the cask conditioned IPA, perhaps her all time favorite beer style. Next, we look to the food. Again Suzanne stays true to form and asks for clam chowder. In the past it has been hit or miss. Obviously some places open a can and "Voilà, bon appétit!" At special places like The Press Room in Portsmouth, New Hampshire, they take the time to make it themselves with a flair for fresh ingredients and an individual touch like rosemary or roasted red potatoes. Here at The Pint, as I expected, the chowder is created with artistry and thoughtfulness. The bacon is house-made, for starters. How many kitchens take time to do that? The Pint makes its own sausages, too. C'mon! But that's not enough. This cup of white, steaming, buttery, peppery, briny, smoky bivalve stew gets its cream base from some happy cows who live nearby. The potatoes are local and the clams are from the nearest coast. If you like New England clam chowder, then you are going to love clam chowder made with actual New England ingredients.

We then ask for the sausage on the Ploughman's Special, but find the popular item has been sold out. That's what happens when you want your pigs from New Hampshire and make the sausage yourself. People enjoy it and order a lot of it and pretty soon you can't make enough. Disappointment is brief and we settle for the regular Ploughman, which is Vermont cheddar cheese, fresh crusty bread, a house-made dill pickle and house-made whole grain mustard. Did I say settled? No, this little bread board clears out fast.

Then we move on to a burger and a salad. The burger is made with Shelburne-raised, grass-fed beef. We add Vermont cheddar, mushrooms, onions, and peppers as well as house-made ketchup and mayo. Oh my! In front of Suzanne is the Asian peanut noodle salad, extremely tasty and a compliment to the grilled beef on my plate, so we trade halfway through.

We are very happy with our food, but the decision, aside from the chowder, was very difficult for me as I searched the menu for local foods. From Hadley dairy and nearby beef to vegetables from Ashfield and Sunderland, carrots and potatoes from South Deerfield and Whatley—the names go on like a map of western Massachusetts. The Pint is of the land, by the land and yes, for the land, as they turn their waste into compost that enriches the soil where the roots of their food grow.

Atlas Farm, Enterprise Farm, Winter Moon Organics, and literally dozens of others supply The Pint with seasonal foods reflected in the changing menu. Among those farms is one tended by The Pint's owner, Alden Booth, in nearby Gill. A cursory search for information on Booth reveals the image of a man on a bicycle with a basket of fresh vegetables riding a few miles to work at his restaurant. Nothing else really adds much to that picture. His values are reflected in detail at his brewpub. In fact, I spot an old-fashioned bicycle mounted above the bar, evergreen bows and holiday lights stung through the spokes. Also, The Pint offers a discount for every mile of automobile travel their customers replace with a bicycle.

After some errant messages and missed opportunities, I finally got to speak with Booth. We met at The Pint for the release of a special beer called Baby Rhino Session IPA. On this night Booth and Brewer Chris Sellers tapped a cask of this 100 percent local malt and hops beer that was low in alcohol and high in flavors. Both of those features kept my glass refilled.

This place is as near the perfect embodiment of a sustainable business as I can find. Yet, they still buy stuff from the global supply chains. Coffee, for one, though it's roasted locally. And yes, most of the malt and hops in their beer. Still, it seems they have thought of ways to keep the dollars flowing locally that other places have not.

For a long time they didn't take credit or debit cards. Paying for local products with a corporate card sends a portion of the money into distant pockets. Yet, lately even this model of Main Street commerce will accept payment with plastic. Booth says the change happened reluctantly. "People now, all they're doing is using debit cards, and they have to go across the street and pay some transaction fee. We thought that's not cool. Back then people had more cash."

As a community, merchant fees on the use of plastic saps the economy and makes it more difficult to muster the capital for an expanded local supply network. On the other hand, paying with cash keeps every penny in the hand where it was placed. So, next time you're shopping conscientiously, take a minute to walk into your bank, swap small chat with a human teller and spread your green where it has the best chance of keeping your community strong. And when you do that in Greenfield, MasterCard® won't get a piece of this great brewpub. Instead it will remain The People's Pint.

Yet, the plastic thing is a minor setback—a compromise with an imperfect monetary system. Over the years, the direction of The Pint has been forward. "We're still heading in the direction we'd like to be going," Booth says. "We started it because back in the mid-90s, in Greenfield, there were only places that had basic burgers and French fries. There really wasn't a lot going on. There was home and there was work, but there just weren't any places to go and hang out. And we wanted to brew beer. We weren't thinking a lot about food at the time. Now we do a lot more food because we've really gotten into supporting local farms. That's been fun."

In essence, Booth got into business at the right time. A movement toward local farm fresh had been seeded and was about to take root. Part of the success of that movement has to go to The People's Pint for carrying local and seasonal foods from the beginning. Booth says, "Back then there wasn't a big push for the local thing, but immediately we said let's see what's available from around here.

Swiss chard quesadilla, Booth recalls, was an early menu item. "People were like 'what is Swiss chard?' It's amazing how far people have come in the last ten to fifteen years. It's great to feel this big surge. Now it's not very radical at all. People have told us we got them thinking. For instance, right from the start we said we're not going to serve tomatoes years round. We're only going to serve them when I have them on my farm and that's it for about two months. Right from the start we've been stubborn about that. People thought it was ridiculous."

Strong locavore sentiment among customers has spilled over from the kitchen into the brewery. "As soon as we could find barley," Booth says, they started using it. "It wasn't being grown around here back then. Neither were hops. Vermont has a long history of hops but hadn't done any hops in a long time. The first thing we could find local to put in our beer was probably honey. Grain and hops weren't available until the last five years. It just wasn't around. We take everything we can from Valley Malt."

"We use about 40 percent local in our food," Booth says. "In our beer, it's about 5 percent." Farm to glass is here and now, but it doesn't yet approach farm to plate.

Great Beer is Everywhere

It's gotten to be a good habit. Wherever I am going, I get online and search draft menus in that area. Usually it doesn't take long to find what I'm looking for, especially around here where I know the usual suspects. Today we are dropping one of our children off at a friend's house in Northampton for a sleep-over. The other child is also away for the afternoon. We have a window of opportunity. We have a target in mind. Every day an adventure.

Heading to Northampton always cranks up the anticipation. Good food, a walkable town, interesting architecture, lively culture and the Northampton Brewery, the oldest brewpub in New England. The sun is trying to bust free from the rain clouds on this early autumn day as we head toward the entrance, a nondescript painted brick wall with a door. Big smiles erupt on our faces. We know what to expect. Inside is far brighter than it has been out in the rain. The lightly stained wood bar and walls feel warm and inviting. We saddle up to a barstool and read the draft board, even though I already know what I want—Four Star Hop Harvest.

At 2:30 p.m. on a Saturday, our happily busy bartender takes the time to explain what we are getting. This is a brew based on the recipe of an earlier pale ale called Four Star Harvest Ale. Only this one gets kicked up by dry hopping with a liberal dose of locally grown Galaxy, Centennial and Nugget. A golden yellow color, clear around the edges but hazy overall, this beer gets in the nose like the spray from a peeling orange. It has a fruity, citrusy zing and an upfront bitterness that leaves me wanting more. The malt stands on its own in this hop-infused glass, providing backbone and a hint of soft French bread for balance. With my second Hop Harvest in front of me, my collaborator checks out the menu. Lo and behold, this place also includes fresh produce grown within ten miles at a place called J.O.E.'s Farm. According to the brewery website, this food is sustainably grown without pesticides, but right now we stick with the liquid feast.

RUNNING WATER

by Suzanne LePage

Suzanne LePage teaches land use planning and is the director of the Campus Sustainability Project Center at Worcester Polytechnic Institute.

There is a small dam on the Mousam River in Springvale, Maine, where we lived for five years starting in 1999. We walked by it almost daily. At the time, the stroller was our way of enticing the wee ones to take naps, and I worked three blocks away. Walking was our major mode of transportation, and the neighborhood was well suited for it. In less than ten minutes, we could reach my office, the library, a pharmacy, a couple of convenience stores, an ice cream shop, a hairdresser, a playground, a river trail, and a few other amenities, but no brewpub.

When a rectangular building right on the water near that dam went up for sale, we fantasized about opening one there. We'd call it the Pour House—inspired by the water pouring over the top of that dam. This was one of many food-related businesses we'd dreamed up and planned out—usually while drinking a pint or two (or three).

Although Worcester, Massachusetts needed a good drive-through gourmet breakfast spot in 1996 and Portsmouth, New Hampshire would have certainly supported a vegetarian buffet centered on the baked potato in 1998, we knew enough about the food business to know that we did not want to spend all of our time there. Still, it's hard to resist the daydream. While we drank our Gritty's and Geary's, that we could bring home in six-packs from the corner store in Springvale in 2001, we imagined sitting on a deck over the Mousam River, listening to that universally-loved sound: running water.

I spend a lot of time thinking about how water moves through various natural and anthropogenic systems. I even wrote a paper in graduate school about brewery wastewater. When I shared it with a Massachusetts brewer whose production was stressing their on-site septic system, I was encouraged by his excitement. It's true that some things you do in an academic environment have real application outside the lecture halls. So, to write this chapter, I started with the wastewater paper, but I ran into a few surprises and learned a little bit more about my favorite beverage.

THE MAIN INGREDIENT

Beer is mostly water, usually at least 90 percent, with the remainder being alcohol and fermentation byproducts, so it makes sense that the characteristics of the water will have an impact on the quality of the beer. In fact, there are many varieties of beer that became unique and expressive because of the kind of water in their region. For example, Burton-on-Trent styles are known as hoppy ales, originally brewed along the River Trent in Staffordshire, England, while the waters of Bohemia in the Czech Republic have been known to produce the rounder, maltier flavor of the Bohemian Pilsner.

What is it about the water that changes from region to region? Well, water is not just two hydrogen atoms bonded to an oxygen atom. That bond is fairly weak, actually, and the hydrogens often tear away and bond with other elements that the water is exposed to, which is why water is such a good solvent, and why it so readily picks up minerals and other constituents as it travels through the landscape. Carbon is an element that's prevalent in nature, and it gets along pretty well with a group of oxygen atoms, often in the form of carbonate (CO_3^{-2}) and that net negative charge attracts hydrogen ions (H^+), forming a variety of other compounds depending on how many hydrogens join the party. Sulfur has a similar relationship with water, creating sulfates (SO_4^-). Other common elements in the natural world that mix and match in an aqueous solution include Calcium (Ca), Nitrogen (N), Phosphorus (P), Iron (Fe), and Magnesium (Mg). They all have impacts on the flavor and quality of the beer.

Mashing is the first step in the brewery, and the process where the quality of the water is the most important. Essentially, the idea is to extract the fermentable sugars from the grain and transport it to the wort. Grain is organic matter, with phosphorus being one of the major elements. We can generally consider malt phosphates as the organic matter that we want to break down. Positively-charged ions in the brew water, like calcium, will have an impact on this process. Calcium and phosphates are attracted to each other, and will form solids that precipitate out of the wort, driving off the sugar compounds as well as hydrogen ions. The sugar compounds become the basis of the wort, and the increase in hydrogen lowers the pH, which enhances the mash process since it is optimized when the pH is around 5.2.

Other minerals have similar impacts on the process, and the minerals are also considered good nutrients for the yeast, which will help the fermentation process later.

Since water always comes into contact with the natural landscape—both above and below ground—it picks up different levels of these various constituents, and the water takes on a characteristic "profile" for a region. The mineral content in water impacts how "hard" or "soft" the water is considered. Higher mineral content results in hard water and is generally considered better for lighter ales and beers where you want a strong presence of hops. Lower mineral content will typically produce a maltier brew. The mineral content in water coming directly from a natural source will also vary from place to place; even time of year can have an impact.

Of course, time of year also impacts our taste buds. In autumn, I am a slave to the Oktoberfest. In winter, the darker German styles seem to take my interest. In spring, I look for hoppy aromas, and in summer, I want a good, solid, drinkable beer—something that travels well to the beach, tastes good after working in the field, and matches the fireside music at night. My top three picks: Tuckerman's Pale Ale (which Jonathan writes about in Chapter 9), Sierra Nevada Pale Ale (obviously not part of the New England beer terrain), and Harpoon IPA.

When you pour a Harpoon IPA (if you bother to pour), you get a nice hint of hop aroma, but not the distinctive blast that you get with some of these newer hoppier selections. I love those aromas in the spring because it complements the freshness in the air and the newness of the garden soil, but I don't necessarily want it every time I open one in the warmer months. The color is what you imagine when you think of thirst-quenching beer. Darker than those light, wheat-based brews that most people label as their summer selections, but not dark enough to make you think of harvesting. And the taste? Just good beer—slightly complex so that it's not boring, but not so strong in flavor that you have to limit your intake. On a hot summer day, who wants to worry about limiting intake? Also, it doesn't hurt that you can find it almost anywhere, and you can get a good deal when you purchase a loose case (which is also less packaging). I guess it just tastes like home. Maybe it's in the water.

Waters of the New England Beer Terrain

Do New England waters offer brewers a distinct profile as the basis for their craft? The answer depends on the physical landscape and the biochemical processes that take place in the region. Are they the same everywhere or is there significant variation?

The whole science of categorizing an area based on its physical patterns and processes (known as physiography) classifies New England as its own distinct area—officially one of twenty-five provinces in the US. So something about this area makes it unique. It could simply be considered part of the same region as the rest of the Appalachian Mountains because of the primary rock types: ancient metamorphic (schist, gneiss, slate, and marble) and igneous (mostly granite). But New England differs from the more southern parts of the mountain range because of water's impact here so long ago. The entire region at one time was glaciated, and when those glaciers moved and melted, any loosely bound rock was moved, crushed, and mixed with other loose material—eventually depositing itself on the landscape and now referred to as glacial till. Some of that till is now the basis of highly prized topsoil—especially in the Connecticut River Valley, which of course, is where Valley Malt is located.

All of that glacial action also made the topography and geology within the New England landscape very diverse. There are mountains—the highest is Mount Washington at 6,288 feet above sea level, and there are some others reaching around 3,500 feet, but most of the land in the White and Green Mountains are between 500 and 1,500 feet above sea level. Then there are undulating hilly areas almost everywhere else, except for where it gets flat near the beaches of Massachusetts, Rhode Island, and Connecticut.

The United States Geological Service (USGS) conducted a study on the types of rocks and ecosystems throughout New England and their impact on water quality. They defined seven different bedrock units, and if you look at a map of them, there is no obvious dominant type and most subregions have at least two to three different bedrock units, except for Cape Cod, which is practically just a collection of sand dunes. So, the lack of a common geology makes it highly unlikely for there to be consistency in the mineral content of the water in New England.

We also do not have a common water source. New England's water supply is, for the most part, very decentralized. Most rural and suburban residents and small businesses draw directly from their own groundwater sources via private wells. In New Hampshire, Hill Farmstead credits the farm's well water with the high quality of their beer. Most southern towns have their own water districts, drawing from groundwater or small reservoirs, providing minimal treatments (most often disinfection), and distributing it nearby to the more densely settled places. Therefore, water does not generally get used very far from its source—with at least one notable exception.

WATER ON RESERVE

Heading west along Route 9 from Worcester about midway to Northampton, and thirty miles from any sizable town, a nondescript sign marks the entrance to the Quabbin Reservoir. Prior to 1927, the north end of the Swift River Valley was well stocked with small farms and water-powered mills. Today, the five towns in that thirty-eight square mile area no longer exist. After everyone was forced to move out, a dam was built. Then the bowl-shaped valley slowly filled with more than 400 billion gallons of water destined for the sinks and toilets of greater Boston.

The Quabbin is famous in Massachusetts. Some view it as a magnificent engineering feat; some a bold pro-active move to secure safe drinking water for a growing metropolis; and some see a politically motivated process that benefited the rich to the east at the expense of the poor in the west. There are still a few folks around who remember their families needing to move, there are various books on the topic, and the history is well-documented at the Visitor's Center.

However, the Quabbin wasn't the first major dam and reservoir to be built for Boston. In 1897, homes were evacuated, graves moved, churches and schools relocated, and roads and railroad tracks closed about thirty miles east of the Quabbin. The Wachusett Dam was built on the south branch of the Nashua River, and now holds back a 4,135-acre reservoir in the towns of Boylston, West Boylston, Sterling, and Clinton. By the time it was filled and operational, more than a decade later, the future need for even more water on reserve was recognized, and plans for the Quabbin began. Boston needed the water because it was growing, but the net result was loss of farms. This serves as only one example of the pressures on farmland in this region.

Today, fifty-one communities get their drinking water from the Quabbin and Wachusett reservoirs, although fifteen of those only partially rely on that water source and three of them tap in for emergencies only. The reservoirs are managed in a linked system operated by the Massachusetts Water Resources Authority, or MWRA. Some of the water leaves the Quabbin to the south for use in South Hadley, Chicopee, and Wilbraham. The rest travels east through the Wachusett Reservoir and on to treatment in Marlborough. From there, it is distributed to the rest of the MWRA communities. Within that area, there may be less than a dozen breweries using it in their brew.

On the Massachusetts Brew Guild's map of breweries, the closest to the Quabbin Reservoir is Amherst Brewing Company, but Amherst has its own water district, drawing from local small reservoirs and underground. Same for nearby Northampton—different water district, but also using both groundwater and surface water. East of the Quabbin, lies Wormtown, but Worcester gets its water from reservoirs just outside the city. You don't start tasting the Quabbin in a brew until you get to Framingham—home of Jack's Abby Brewing. Framingham is about thirty miles away. Not as local as most water in New England.

The other breweries in towns served by the Quabbin-Wachusett system include Mystic Brewery in Chelsea, Night Shift Brewing Company and Idle Hands Craft Ales in Everett, and three in Boston—Harpoon, Boston Beer Company (Sam Adams), and the newest, Trillium, which opened in 2013. Even though the water travels from central Massachusetts, most of the beer made with that water never leaves the Boston area. The only ones I could find at Yankee Spirits in Sturbridge were Jack's Abby and Harpoon. Aha! Maybe it is the water.

After a little investigation, I find out that Harpoon has a second brewery in Windsor, Vermont, so I may be drinking beer from Vermont today. Since they condition their water before brewing, it's probably not the Quabbin that tastes so comforting, but it was the first local craft brewery that awakened my senses to good beer. The visit there with college buddies in the early 1990s for a tour and tasting must have built in a bit of brand loyalty because it's still one of my favorite summer brews.

Having begun the search for Quabbin water in a brew, I can no longer settle for my first impression. I go back to the store and look over the selection from Framingham's Jack's Abby, snag a four-pack of my favorite, Hoponious Union, and hurry home to open and enjoy.

The generous half-liter bottles (slightly more than a pint each) come in a four-pack. Poured into a large mug, it looks crisp and delicious with an airy head. And it tastes as good as it looks. Refreshing and hoppy, it satisfies the urge for the IPA.

According to owner Jack Hendler, "The Quabbin is a really high quality water source for brewing. It's one of the top five water sources in the country." For starters, he says, the Quabbin's water is soft, meaning there is not a lot of mineral content compared with well water, which spends a lot it's time in contact with rock substrates.

"The best water for brewing is one that doesn't leave a profile in the beer," he says. "We know we have to adjust the water to our needs anyway. The pH of the mash is important to the shelf life and the efficiency." The acidity levels of the Quabbin are kept low to prevent absorption of lead, which is present due to an aging delivery system. In order to adjust the pH Hendler will add calcium salt, which has the added benefit of bringing out the flavors of hops—something Jack's Abby does well enough to earn them wide acclaim.

To ensure there are no antimicrobials that could inhibit yeast, such as chlorine, Jack's uses a carbon filter for all their incoming water. The Quabbin is relatively chlorine-free due their use of ozone to supplement the treatment process. Consistent with their clean water source, Jack's uses only their house lager yeast which provides a clean, almost flavorless finish, allowing the high quality, and often local ingredients to shine.

How Much Water?

If beer is 90 percent water, then you need at least 14.4 ounces to make a pint. Surely it takes more water than that to make beer. To get a sense of just how much water the beer terrain consumes, I attempted to find out how many gallons of beer are brewed in New England, but the staggering 2.5 million gallons coming out of Shipyard and the nearly 750,000 gallons at Smuttynose stopped me from going much further. So many small microbreweries to find out about, and also a few giants:

Boston Beer Company (Sam Adams), Harpoon (Boston and Vermont), Shipyard (Portland, Maine) and Anheuser-Busch in Merrimack, New Hampshire. The numbers become so large, they are nearly meaningless to most of us, unless we can equate it to something like how many baseball stadiums all the beer would fill. The numbers, however, aren't really the most important part. What bears consideration is the fact that it takes more water than that to make a beer, and most of it is used to grow the ingredients.

WATER IN

For starters, let's think about the beer-making process and which steps need water. The figure below depicts this process.

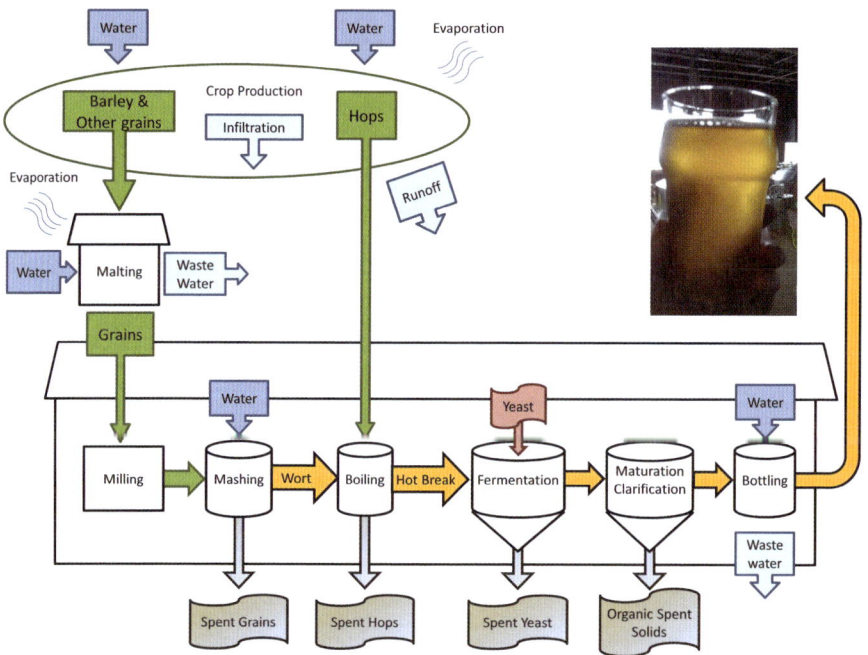

Along this process train, water is a critical input. The sum of all the water needed to make the finished product is often referred to as its water footprint. The source of the water is an important consideration, so footprint science analyzes by where the water originated: green for rain and blue for withdrawals.

Green water is basically rainwater. Only the amount that is taken up by the plants or evaporated is counted. Anything that runs off the field or percolates to the groundwater is considered available for other uses and so is not considered in the footprint. The nice thing about green water is that it doesn't take any external energy to move it around the field or apply it to crops. However, rainfall amounts are not consistently predictable, and there could be atmospheric contaminants—acid rain, lead, mercury, etc.

Blue water refers to anything that is drawn from sources such as reservoirs or groundwater wells. This may be a direct withdrawal or it may come via public water supply systems. It includes water applied to fields for plants, as well as the water used at the brewery.

Does everyone account for these inputs in the same manner? Not necessarily. Also, there are regional differences due to climate, agricultural practices, brewing innovations, and other factors. Global estimates of a beer's water footprint published by the Water Footprint Network and some universities vary from twenty-five to thirty gallons of water per pint of finished beer. So, a major brewing company (SABMiller) partnered with the World Wildlife Federation to study their operations in the Czech Republic and in South Africa. They found that they were using almost twenty-four gallons to brew a pint of beer in South Africa and less than six gallons in the Czech Republic. While not directly related to a prediction for New England craft brewers, a few key points are notable.

First of all, 90-98 percent of the water used in the beer-making process is used to grow the ingredients. This helps explain the drastic difference in water footprints between the two study locations. In short, there is much more irrigation needed to produce beer ingredients in South Africa than in the Czech Republic. So, if you are lucky enough to rely on rainfall to grow your crops, your water footprint will be much lower.

Also, in South Africa, the amount of beer-making ingredients that are imported weigh in at about 30 percent with a corresponding water footprint of about five and a half gallons. Meanwhile, in the Czech Republic, only 5 percent of its ingredients are imported, adding less than one and a half gallons to the footprint. Why do the imported ingredients have a larger footprint? The short answer is that the importing process involves packaging, transportation, and additional energy, and these processes require water. Therefore, the more that your ingredients are sourced locally, the smaller the water footprint.

These findings are good news for the New England beer terrain. We get a lot of rainfall during the growing season, and we are increasingly able to supply our brewers with local ingredients. However, the Czech Republic receives an average rainfall of twenty-six inches each year, with variation in the three years studied between twenty-four and twenty-seven and a half. New England rainfall varies from the coast to the mountains, but it's just about double those values in most areas. So, our farmers may be concerned with too much rain, rather than not enough. Dry periods are needed for grain harvesting, and too much humidity can encourage disease in hops. Because rainfall is rarely predictable and often not received in the right amount at the right time, New England farmers still need to irrigate at times.

So, what about the other 2-10 percent of the water inputs? Although the brewing and bottling processes seemingly need an insignificant amount of water when compared to that needed for crop production, we cannot ignore the amount needed or negate the efforts to conserve. The water inputs for mashing and cleaning are typically blue water, which means that we are tapping into our drinking water supply to get it, and it isn't free, unless you are using your own well water. Public water rates in New England generally range between $3.00 and $9.00 for every 1,000 gallons.

The amount a brewery uses can vary depending upon whether any water conservation practices are in place, but traditional breweries need about six pints of water for every pint of beer brewed. Remember the earlier figures—twenty-five to thirty gallons to make a pint—well, less than a gallon of that is consumed at the brewery. Long Trail Brewing Company, however, needs only about 2.4 pints for every pint brewed. The brewery uses about 20,000 gallons of water per day, which is about as much as they are permitted to withdraw. So, water conservation is not just a feel-good measure, it allows them to make more beer with a limited supply. How do they do it?

First, they recover and re-use water in a few isolated closed-loop systems. The rinse water for bottles is recaptured, filtered, sterilized with ultraviolet light, and then used again to rinse the next batch of bottles. Only a small amount of water needs to be replenished once in a while when water is lost to spills. Also, the bottling process uses a vacuum pump, which needs water to operate. May as well keep re-using the same water for that process, too. And the kegging operation includes cleaning. The final rinse water is recaptured, filtered, sterilized and used to supplement the primary cleaning water for the next batch of kegs. They also recover all the steam from the boiling kettles and condense it. The condensate isn't used to brew, but the heat that gets extracted is used to pre-heat the next batch—cutting down on the time and energy needed to boil.

A big contributor to their conservation efforts? The workers. They are trained to minimize wherever possible, and there are a few operation systems in place to help them do that. It's just Long Trail's philosophy of how they do business, according to Matt Quinlan, Director of Operations, and he has been there for twenty-one years.

WATER OUT

As the beer is being created, there are various stages where water is leaving the system. First, during crop production, any rainwater that is not used by plants will typically find its way to the groundwater table or nearby surface waters, but it often carries fertilizer and sediment with it. Not only does the farmer not want to lose those items, the nearby surface waters where they end up can be harmed by an overabundance of either. So, if it's polluted, it should be treated—the way we would other wastewater.

In the brewery, most of the wastewater is generated in the cleaning process. Equipment needs to be cleaned and rinsed, and so do the bottles and kegs that will carry the beer to the consumer. There is also water lost in some of the brewing by-products. After mashing, the wort is separated from the spent grains, which become wet waste products. The boiling process results in hot break and spent hops—also wet waste. Fermentation produces excess yeast—some of which can be reused for beer production, but typically it's added to the wastewater stream prior to treatment and disposal. Similarly, the maturation and clarification processes result in organic spent solids, which may also be added to the wastewater stream.

Some breweries are able to discharge directly to a municipal wastewater treatment system. Smuttynose Brewing Company in Portsmouth, New Hampshire has this luxury, despite the fact that in 2006, their annual production exceeded the 15,000 barrel threshold of a micro-brew. Still, the city of Portsmouth has simply tacked on a monthly surcharge, which, according to head brewer, David Yarrington, is still cheaper than the investment that would be required to treat their wastewater. As the brewery develops plans to move to a new location in Hampton, Massachusetts, they recognize the likelihood of requiring pre-treatment, and may explore innovative methods to do so.

For those breweries that treat their wastewater, the process may include a combination of physical, chemical, and biological treatment. Physical treatment removes the majority of undissolved solids by screening and gravity sedimentation. Chemical treatment refers to a process, known as flocculation, that removes fine particles and dissolved solids. A chemical additive is introduced, and the wastewater is stirred or agitated to induce the clumping of fine particles that can then be settled out as sludge. Biological treatment involves the introduction of microorganisms to wastewater to aid in the breakdown and removal of organic matter.

Of the 20,000 gallons that Long Trail uses each day, about half of it ends up as wastewater. For treatment, they first pre-separate as much as possible at each stage where wet waste is produced. For example, the yeast, which is a strong waste, is added to their sludge and hauled away. Otherwise, it would require more energy and work to clean the wastewater. Their on-site biological treatment process uses activated sludge, which is essentially a digestive system. With a selection of bacteria effective at digesting waste (heterotrophs), the high organic and nutrient content in wastewater is converted to a semi-solid waste product, which can be coagulated into a sludge that settles out. Then, the effluent is distributed to a leach field for more nutrient removal before percolating through the subsurface and replenishing the groundwater supply.

Yes, this is the same groundwater that is tapped to make the beer in the first place. The closed-loop system is so impressive, they won the Governor's Award for Environmental Excellence in 2009.

What it Means to Be Local

Besides using their own groundwater, Long Trail has also been supporting the use of local ingredients a little bit along the way since the early 1990s when they first planted hops at their Bridgewater, Vermont brewery. However, they consider themselves brewers, not farmers, so they use the limited supply of homegrown hops in small trial batches available only in their tasting room.

In the early fall of 2013, they released a surprise brew—made with Vermont-grown barley that was malted in New England's only malt house. Exciting to see Valley Malt getting more business, and also happy to hear that this batch of Long Trail was available in retail outlets. They also made a Maple Maiboch earlier that year, but it was only available at their brewery and in a few places nearby on draft. Like the geology and water quality, New England is incredibly diverse, and local means a much smaller range than just from within this terrain.

When we visited Doug and Jeff Therrien at the Rock Island Hop Farm in Springvale, Maine, we were excited to drive around our old neighborhood—showing the kids our former walking routes. Not too many changes in the last nine years, although the ice cream shop was no longer there. It had been replaced with the Springvale Publick House—an intriguing little casual restaurant and bar. We were tempted to stop in for a pint, but we knew that Doug and Jeff had some Sebago Brewing Company's Local Harvest on ice for us. They wanted to share it because it featured the hops they grew. It was a limited edition brew—only available in those parts, and only for a short time. In return, we had brought along a Wormtown Hopulence. A little flavor from our part of the New England beer terrain. They liked it, which was impressive, because as it turns out, they really only drink Maine beers—others are not really "local" in their minds. We asked about the beer selection at the Publick House. They have twenty taps offer up some unique selections. However, Doug told us, "I go in there and they always have a new beer on tap they want me try. No thanks. Give me a Maine beer."

Maybe it's because Maine is his home. Maybe it's the ocean breezes. Maybe it's the water.

RENEWABLE BREWING

Beer Terrain

Beer is essentially a fermented tea and as such, as we have seen, uses a lot of water, which must be heated. It's a process requiring large amounts of fuel. The standard methods use imported, finite fuel supplies such as oil and gas. In the case of The Barrington Brewery, a rooftop solar heat exchanger works in tandem with a gas burner to heat the brew. "We put in solar hot water in 2006," says Andrew Mankin, cofounder and head brewer. He notes that Barrington was the first brewer in the Northeast to heat their water with the sun and "one of the biggest systems in the state for a while."

Considering this is New England, and the sun hardly seems to make an appearance for most of six months during the expansive November to April cold season, solar heated water may not seem like the most effective fuel source. During the summer, in most cases, both commercial and residential hot water use decreases. Much more hot water is used in the Northeast during cold weather, when the sun is weakest. In Great Barrington, Massachusetts, however, this brewery in the Berkshires tends to be much busier from late spring through fall. As a result, hot water usage corresponds with the strong solar season.

Mankin says when the weather heats up, the tourists from Boston, New York, and New Jersey begin to head his way for some mountain air, the scenic landscape, outdoor theaters, and the Tanglewood concert series. Foliage season tends to mark the end of the busy time, just after the autumn equinox. "We get the leaf peepers," Mankin says, appreciatively. After that they rely on the locals to stay open and the gas to heat the water. "We've tried to create an environment where everyone feels comfortable," he says, adding, "We couldn't survive without the local support."

Having opened their doors in 1996, Mankin and his partner Gary Happ were ten years in when they decided to expand and provide banquet facilities. This meant a new building and they saw the opportunity to make their environmental footprint a little smaller. "When we first sat down with the engineer, it was a little discouraging," he says. "The numbers don't look great."

Into its sixth season of use, the initial investment will still take some time until the cost is covered by the savings. "It's an eight- to ten-year payback," Mankin says. "There are not a lot of rebates for commercial hot water. We took advantage of a tax credit, but not a lot of money coming back as an incentive." An investment that won't pay off for a decade requires foresight, and perhaps a motivating factor that has nothing to do with financial profit. "We were saving for all these things, you know. We wanted to have a nice project, nice carpet, nice doors. At some point you've got to put your money where your mouth is and we saw it as a chance to cut down on our fossil fuels and be more sustainable."

But why hot water? Most solar power being put in these days is for electricity production. "In brewing, you use a lot of water," Mankin says. "Once we did it, we knew right away it was worth it. It's pretty cool to watch it work and see how much hot water you can get. It's working well. We save two-thirds the cost of gas heating. Instead of heating water from fifty degrees, we get it at 120 or even 160. When it's going good, you don't have to do much."

Then there are the fringe benefits, such as publicity. "We use it. We use it on our logo on six-packs. People talk about it." The solar water system also got them some free print advertising in the form of newspaper and magazine stories. Being first is a newsworthy accomplishment. Another benefit was unexpected. Turns out heating the water outside the building is a bonus. "In summer, because we're not running the gas kettle as much, we use less AC." Mankin explains, "I'd say we save about a quarter of that cost." So not only do they get hot water, but they save electricity, too.

While solar hot water is by far Barrington's biggest investment in sustainability, they don't stop there. "Since the beginning we've always tried to use local ingredients." In both the brewery and the kitchen, seasonal farm products are in use. Yet, Mankin is skeptical about the prospects of ever replacing long distance supplies. "The hard reality is, in the off season, there's not a lot of local. Even though we get our fresh raspberries and strawberries in season, as well as asparagus, we don't claim to be farm to table. It's just not practical to do it all year, but we do our best."

Turns out, he's underselling what they actually do. With a little prodding he admits to much more. "We're carrying local cheeses now. We have free range chicken dinners . . . a quarter of a roast chicken. We get our lettuce from nearby Equinox Farm. We use a lot of local produce in our banquets." Still, there's more. "We've had a grass-fed burger and steak for ten years from a New England co-op. That has been really good." They continue to sell both conventionally raised beef and the local stuff side-by-side, charging $1.50 more for the local. A lot of people seem to think the premium price is well worth it. The New England beef "has become close to 50 percent of all the burgers we sell." As for Mankin, the taste test is over. He knows what he likes. "I will only eat the grass-fed now. There's more flavor and less fat."

From a farm just over the New York state line, he says, "We get really nice fresh tomatoes. They're so good. We slice them up for salad and sandwiches and make a ratatouille. With the seconds we make sauce that we freeze and serve it with pasta specials in the winter." No wonder the locals are loyal supporters. Local energy. Local foods.

There is the understated Mankin, one minute saying local can't be used year round, and the next, explaining how his brewpub goes a step further than most restaurants by actually taking the time and freezer space to preserve the harvest. "There's nothing wrong with the seconds," he says, humbly. "The farmer can't get full price for them, but they taste great; just not pretty." So, he's a thrifty Yankee, too. Time and again, in these pages, sustainability has boiled down to old-fashioned frugality.

Naturally, Barrington Brewery uses local ingredients in their beer, as well. "We grow our own hops," Mankin says. "We grow enough to do two or three batches. We're also working toward bringing in cask conditioned beer. Hops could play into that. We'd put them right in the cask. Everyone wants to grow hops. It's the hot thing right now. I've been growing hops for twenty-five years, even back when I was a homebrewer. We grow Chinook and Nugget and get Cascade from someone nearby." He wishes there were more available. "I'd like to see local hop growing get a little bigger," but he knows it's not easy. "It's definitely a labor of love."

For one thing, he says, local hops don't taste exactly the same as their West Coast counterparts. Local Cascade may not have the same bite as the stuff shipped in from across the continent, but much like those tomato 'seconds', these hops still taste really good. "It's a matter of matching beer style with the hops we have," Mankin says. "It's important to showcase the hops, not try to imitate styles that are suitable elsewhere. It tastes different out here."

New England ingredients are not imitations, even if they wanted to be. They are original, vibrant, full of surprises and still haven't reached their full potential.

One of the beers Barrington makes with their own hops is called Farmer's Ale. This beer also contains malt grown in northern Maine by potato farmers who like barley's soil-improving properties in rotation with the main crop. This grain is malted by industry giant Canada Malt. Mankin says it has more of a caramel flavor than the Midwestern variety. But none of the regional ingredients make a major dent in Barrington's supply. So, why bother? Mankin says, "I personally like doing it. Our customers have come to appreciate it, too. When we first opened, we did an all organic beer and people didn't care that much. Now people are a lot more aware. They've also evolved in what they drink. Flavors like Oktoberfest are bigger. Spring bock used to stay around forever. Now it's gone pretty fast. People are willing to try new styles and flavors." That includes the distinctive character of regional terroir.

FORESTS OF THE NORTH

Jackson, NH

October, 1999

Twice we missed the turn because of hungry darkness. Then, climbing the steep road to the top of Black Mountain for our night's meal and bed, our poor Chevy strained and the headlights faded as we slowly rode up and up.

I nibbled the rim of a foam cup with a swallow of coffee as cold as space. My collaborator flicked a finger on the edge of our useless map. We both stared ahead, up the forest sleeve, enveloped in darkness.

Emerging suddenly in front of Eagle Mountain House, the wheels cracked on gravel the way my knees crunched when I got out of my seat. At the trunk, I extracted a suitcase and single malt whisky old enough to vote. The October night air made my breath wag in front me like steam from a city subway grate. I stood for a moment feeling small under the distant glimmer of indifferent stars.

A whiff of wood smoke perfume brought my gaze to the appealing blush of tavern windows. As much for the bed, we were here for what the tavern had on tap. Checking into our room first, I left the whisky on the night table and walked arm in arm with Suzanne down the hall and down the elevator to the nearly empty barroom. We seem to have this historic hotel almost to ourselves. With each step, the carpeted floorboards let out a deep, but muffled belch, as if they already had enough beer. With the Red Sox playing the Yankees on the lone, small screen TV above the old dark wood bar, I decided to grab a pair of padded bar stools that featured stay-awhile back rests.

The barkeep slung a white towel over his shoulder and raised his eyebrows at us. The facial gesture caused ripples all the way up to the top of his bald head, as if his dark eyes had been tossed like pebbles to break the surface tension. I ordered a pair of Tuckerman's Pale Ales and smiled when he placed the foaming brews on coasters in front of us. As we watched the Sox game on mute and sipped our beers, the fire crackled in the wall and the only other couple in the place laughed warmly in a corner booth. Soon, we needed more beer and wordlessly, the barman supplied it.

When Suzanne got up to find the ladies' room, I took an interest in some of the old photos framed on a nearby wall. Several depicted the story of the hotel's evolution since 1879, including a fire that led to a whole new building being erected. In the early years, a few golf holes were established due to the popularity of the new sport, adding another activity to a list that included trout fishing, hiking, snowshoeing and skiing, not to mention taking in the spectacular views of the Presidential Range to the northwest.

What a great way to celebrate our recent wedding! For our honeymoon it was telling that we drove in a grand loop all over New England, stopping to visit friends, family, and brewpubs. We were awed by the White Mountains, crossed the Connecticut River several times, hit Providence, Boston, Portland, Brattleboro, and Keene. We made easy friends and took a great number of walks. After that Grand Hotel, we headed west through the mountains on the Kancamagus Highway to

Vermont where we found breweries like Jasper Murdock's Alehouse and McNeill's, but it's New Hampshire's Tuckerman Brewing Co. that sticks out in my memory. Tuckerman Ravine, which is situated on the flank of Mount Washington, is a precipitous wall that descends at a 55-degree angle. The ravine was carved out by glacial erosion and is depicted, with accompanying skiers, on the namesake beer's 12-ounce bottle. That whole summer we bought Tuckerman's by the case and used the boxes to start our campfires. By the sea or at our circa 1700 house with the field of waving hay, wherever we had friends and music and starry skies, we'd bring some Tuck's along. Something about spending a lot of time outdoors brings peace to the soul. That reverence is shared by Tuckerman's founders, Nik Stanciu and Kirsten Neves.

Located in the foothills of the White Mountains, Tuckerman Brewing Co. is surrounded by imposing peaks and millions upon millions of woodland acres. Still small, but growing, these guys remain mindful of the resources they consume. Beginning with the forests they love, their concern is manifest in their choices when it comes to purchasing supplies. Every bottle of beer they sell leaves the brewery with twenty-three others packed into a cardboard casebox. A successful bottling line uses a lot of trees.

One available option is to ignore nagging concern and buy the cheapest product available, but that's not how it's done at Tuckerman's. Right down to where the boxes come from, decisions are not made on price point alone. Paying more for something that is not destructive to the environment makes more sense than squeezing pennies from their profit margin. These brewers don't operate with consumer mentalities where the only cost that matters is the dollar amount. Instead they ask, what is the source and where will this end up? Asking those two questions takes into account the whole cost of a product, including which side of the sustainability ledger they're on.

When it came time to order boxes, they found a company in nearby Auburn, Maine that makes them from trees harvested under the guidelines of the Sustainable Forestry Initiative. SFI is an independent certifier of wood sourcing. They allow companies that meet their criteria to label products as SFI-approved and therefore harvested responsibly. International Paper, a company that got a reputation over the years of being less than environmentally benign, is putting some of their enormous buying power toward improving forest management. According to SFI literature, consumer demand for products that go a little easier on the world's woodlands drives companies toward forests under sustainable management harvesting plans. In Maine alone, seven million acres of the boundless forest are certified by SFI.

The Tuckerman's case boxes are manufactured by International Paper, a very large corporation with forest holdings all over the world, especially in Brazil. However, their headquarters are in the next state to the east. "We'd used a couple different suppliers in the past," Neves says. "IP had this forestry program. That tipped the decision in their favor."

It helps that they are local, too. "We like to use local suppliers as much as we can," Neves says. "We get local labels." She explains why patronizing area businesses is a better option than finding the cheapest, no matter where they're located. "Local doesn't require a lot of shipping. We're all connected. Hopefully it comes back around full circle among local suppliers."

Tuckerman's base malt also has a local component. It features Maine grown barley that serves as a rotation crop for potato farmers. Their water trickles down from the White Mountains and leaves a fresh and clean mark on a bottle of Tuck's. The fuel for the steam kettle is biodiesel, which does a lot less harm than petroleum. If biofuel spills, it is essentially vegetable oil and will degrade as such. When it burns, it smells like a restaurant. Petroleum emits deadly fumes. So biofuel is better for the atmosphere. "It costs more," she says, "but it's important to reduce petroleum use." Yet, Neves has no illusions. Even with all Tuckerman's does, she knows it is a small step. She says, "At this point we haven't done as much as we hope to do."

These decisions make a difference. Instead of things getting worse, they can actually get better. Neves says, "It's just a mindset we try to stick with in our business practices."

FINDING THE SPIRIT

I cross the Mystic River without ever laying eyes on it from where I sit in the rumbling commuter rail car heading north out of Boston. The landscape that is visible out my window suffers cinder block buildings and massive reclamation yards piled with crushed refrigerators and stoves. Smoking delivery trucks seethe through the streets and everywhere trash gathers on the corners, along the walls, in the weeds and in the chain link fences. Since stepping through the doors of South Station, having arrived from Worcester via bus, I'd hardly noticed anything else except the Styrofoam cups, plastic bags and other detritus of neurotic society.

I am on a mission that began where I was born, in the formerly rural town of Sturbridge, Massachusetts, sixty miles west of Boston. Having hatched a plan to live the life we want, Suzanne and I were discussing the potential for a book about beer made with local grain and hops as we drove to Pioneer Brewing Company for a pint. We considered the concept of 100 percent local beer, and I rued the lack of local yeast, wondering aloud if there were any viable brewing yeasts living in the New England landscape, as yet undiscovered. After all, commercial brewing yeast carefully cultivated and kept pure in sterile laboratories all trace their roots to some wild strain in the distant past.

Pioneer Brewing is housed in a barn at Hyland Orchard. A small truck, painted with the words Mystic Brewery, was parked in the loading bay. I knew the name from the list of Valley Malt BSA members.

Walking into the tap room, I saw a man with a Mystic Brewery T-shirt enjoying a Pioneer Pale Ale. Introducing myself, he turned out to be Mystic founder Bryan Greenhagen. He was there to brew a batch of beer with the Pioneer equipment, then truck it back to the Mystic fermentorium in Chelsea, Massachusetts. I began to ask him about his use of local malt, and in the process explained the concept of the book I had in mind. The conversation returned to yeast. The questions I had posed to Suzanne, just moments earlier, were answered by Greenhagen. Yes, there is such a thing as local brewing yeast, and Greenhagen has painstakingly cultivated it from wild yeast living on the skin of an organic plum.

In reference to the mainstream yeast supply, Greenhagen pointed out that terroir is nowhere to be found. "Everyone knows grains are homogenized. There's no terroir left there, but yeast is homogenized, too."

With his beer break over, Greenhagen had to return to Chelsea, but he invited me to visit and have a taste of what his indigenous Massachusetts yeast could do, which is how I got here, at an open air train stop under a billboard near a highway overpass, still five blocks away from my destination on this hot and humid afternoon.

The little city of Chelsea steams with midsummer and the faces of the boys on the basketball court glisten in the sun. I stay to the shady side of the street, but the harbor breeze can't seem to penetrate this warren of block buildings. Now I've reached a freshly painted, windowless place with a tiny sign on the metal door that tells me I'm here. Inside is a warehouse space with high ceilings and boxy fermentation tanks that make neat rows in the middle of the concrete floor.

In this urban setting, where the only wild plants to be found grow in sidewalk cracks, rooting through road sand and tiny bits of decaying trash, at least there is a taste of the countryside. Greenhagen is telling me about it. A very fine powdery stuff exists on the skin of fruit. You have seen it on grapes and blueberries, probably so many times that you now overlook it. Polish a grape and you are wiping it off. This is yeast, and it is waiting for an opening—in a sort of hibernation—so it can eat.

After my trek, I am feeling the heat and in need of a refreshing beverage so much so that I am having a tough time with my note-taking. Fortunately, the digital voice recorder Velcroed to my sleeve has me covered. It's no fault of Greenhagens' that I am having difficulty with my focus. He's giving me the information I came to get, and I only just walked in the door, but every step along the way I've been thinking about my first mouthful of fermented goodness. I guess you could call it a case of beer fever.

Then we come to a stainless steel box on short legs with a spigot at the bottom. This is it. Greenhagen squirts the nozzle with grain alcohol then sets it aflame with a long handled lighter. A small glass catches the liquid as he pours, and then the disinfection process is repeated. He holds the glass out for us to examine. It is thick, like a smoothie, and brownish red. His expression shows a mix of amused satisfaction and mild disappointment. This beer—called Vinland One—was served up at the Summerville Summer Fest a couple days earlier. Greenhagen recalls, "People were getting thick glasses of murky liquid, asking 'What is this?'" Then he smiles and adds that when they tasted it, "Everyone said, 'Hmm, interesting.'"

Now it's my turn. I get dark fruit and booziness almost like a rum raisin aspect, but there is a bready malt that reminds me this is beer. "Hmm, interesting," I say before I can stop myself.

Greenhagen just nods and asks, "Can you taste the plum?" I sip again. Yes, that raisiny flavor is plum-like as well, or maybe dark cherries without the sweetness. There's no actual plum in there at all, he says. The flavor is from the yeast that had been living on a plum at an organic orchard in Massachusetts. I sip again and get a honey blossom aroma with suggestions of bitter greens and wild herbs.

"It's good," I tell him.

He wants to show me something else. I follow towards the far wall where he has set aside space for his yeast cultivating work, including an incubator. Here is where he cultivated the plum yeast he calls Winnisimit. Then, when he had enough viable yeast cells, Greenhagen pitched them into several containers of dissolved malt sugar.

When yeast, known in the world of science as Saccharomyces, or sugar eater, does its thing, out comes alcohol and carbon dioxide. After that, it is a process of elimination. Smell the results. If it smells good, taste it. If it tastes bad, discard it and keep those with potential. Then ferment another set of sugar waters from the good yeast in the previous test, and so on until what is left is one tasty and . . . interesting concoction.

"We've never had one come out wonderful on the first try," says Greenhagen, "but we go from there to isolate colonies, stack them out on petri plates. We make hundreds of twelve-ounce beers. Most we don't even taste because they smell bad. Cultivating yeast from the wild takes a really long time and there's a little serendipity involved."

For certain, Greenhagen relies more on his background than luck. Having earned a doctorate in microbiology, he did post-graduate work at MIT in nearby Cambridge. Then he went to work for a company researching the science behind flavor. Along the way, he learned that in order to get a good fermentation, organic fruits have to be used. "Yeast culture has to start with organic," he says. "It doesn't work with grocery store stuff."

He learned something else when the economy went into a tailspin and he lost his job.

He says for himself and a lot of others, "The last recession was a death blow to the notion that a big company was going to take care of you. It's no less risky than failing on my own." He adds that working for himself offers the extra advantage of possibly doing something fulfilling. So with eyes wide open he followed his own path here. Inspiration came from a YouTube video where it was said that Belgian brewers get their yeast from the fields. Greenhagen thought, "Wait a minute; I can do that."

Now, after investing $30,000 worth of resources into the work, Mystic Brewing is doing that, fermenting with indigenous yeast. It hasn't quite panned out, business-wise. "We feel misunderstood," he says. "Nobody else is doing this." On the floor, where they will not be too hot in this unairconditioned room, are Bell canning jars covered loosely with foil. Greenhagen picks one up to show me. It's a ferment of blueberry skin yeast that he hopes will be Vinland Two someday. This yeast strain was gathered from Greenhagen's grandparents' farm in Vermont.

For the Greenhagen of the lab and of the farm, time competes with Greenhagen the commercial brewer. Vinland One, on top of the time and expense of cultivating the yeast, took over a month to ferment, whereas their main product, a saison, takes only a week. He says they have hired a "very part-time" corporate financial officer. The advice from this business pro? Too much research, not enough focus on selling product. Greenhagen recalls, "I said, yeah I know, but everyone is asking us to start making yeast. So I guess the R&D will pay off." Still, he admits the need for marketing and says, "I don't know how to talk to people about what we are doing. I'm not a PR kind of person."

Fortunately for Mystic, Belgian beer styles are becoming very popular. When fans of that style find Mystic, everything could work out. More than being of Belgian influence, Greenhagen says, Mystic uses old methods. "It's just the way people used to brew. Belgians are really stubborn and resisted German purity laws." Greenhagen has a lot of respect for the old ways. "That's my personal philosophy," he says. "We should be skeptical of eating things that didn't exist a thousand years ago. Science needs to inform good food."

That goes for beer too. Unfiltered is better, he says. "Beer-wise, we can't make the claim that it's good for you. I personally enjoy drinking beer with yeast in it, the way it was made thousands of years ago. I used to eat processed food and drink homogenized milk and crystal-clear beer and I would feel awful all the time. I feel better after drinking this beer."

I ask him what his long term goals are. "Hopefully," he replies, "we'll be successful enough to keep experimenting."

MYSTICAL LIQUID

Just over a year later, Mystic entered their Vinland Two in the Great American Beer Festival, the biggest and most prestigious in the country. The years of yeast hunting and cultivation garnered appreciation from the judges who hung a gold on this New England native for being the best Indigenous Beer. It seems that Greenhagen, with his scientific background and his appreciation of ancestral brewing methods, discovered one tasty microbe.

In primitive understandings of the brewing process, the work done by yeast was attributed to magic. They could not otherwise explain how a sugary liquid could be changed overnight into something of substance, chock full of essential nutrients including Vitamin B and substantial amounts of protein that, if not for beer, early people would have lacked. Not only that, but the results were mildly alcoholic, imparting an altered reality for the imbiber, dulling the pain of a hard life. Ancient people often associated these magical beverages with religious rites and were careful to pay respect to the spirits that inhabited their brew and made it wholesome and transformative.

But that's just silly. Now we know this "magic" is just a fungus we call yeast. It eats and creates a by-product we happen to like. Simple and easy to understand for enlightened minds of the information age. Yet, is it that simple? How would I know? I've never really looked at it closely.

I decided to dig deeper. But first, I uncork a small bottle of Vinland One that I picked up at Yankee Spirits in Sturbridge. A tasting glass fills with pure white foam that quickly settles into a head of fine suds, amounting to about a third of the volume in the glass. Bubbling below is golden liquid that reveals flashes of reddish orange brown when turned in the light. Bright and clear as a sunny day, this is much more inviting to see than the turbid sample from before.

The aromas are subtle and deep. Rich soil and dry straw. Fresh split hardwood and something unique and beyond metaphor. I guess this is what brewers mean when they say "earthy." It is natural and sets off an elemental fire that makes us want to gather round.

A warming feeling comes from this cool beer. I had put it in the refrigerator for about an hour before opening it and it is not much colder than the recommended serving temperature of 47 degrees. After a swallow, my mouth left dry, I have to admit I've never had another beer like it. The bottle says that Vinland One was named for a historical region found in northeastern America, where the Vikings emerged from the cold barrens of the north and discovered that they could once again create mystic brews like the one you now hold. I find it easy to imagine a settlement forming around beer like this. Wanderers decide to stay because, in the air and on the fruit, there is good yeast.

Reading about brewers yeast, I find that it is one incredible organism. This single-celled microscopic life form can survive with or without oxygen and reproduce with or without sex. Not only does it produce alcohol and carbon dioxide as a by-product, but a whole host of other compounds as well. It doesn't just give beer its bubbles and buzz, but a lot of the flavor, too, a fact that can sometimes be overlooked. Also incredible is the rate of fermentation. Every second, a yeast cell can consume its own mass in sugar, the equivalent of 200 million glucose molecules.

This is going over my head, so I put out a call for help through Suzanne at Worcester Polytechnic Institute. She sent out word that I wanted to learn more about brewing yeast and quickly there were several offers. I decided to call Dr. Reeta Rao who is conducting research to prevent human fungal infections and I am told she has an incubator full of Saccharomyces cerevisiae, or brewing yeast. On the phone, she is inspired. She is, like so many farmers and brewers

I've met, someone who speaks like she finds her work exciting and fulfilling. It takes her no time at all to blow my mind.

Her work focuses on a molecular process called the IAA Synthesis. She explains how it works with natural fermentation environments. "Yeast cells that live on the skin of a grape spend most of their natural life being starved, waiting for the grape to become overripe, for it to open to gain access," she says. The question is, "How does it know there is a wound on the grape? It could be the mechanism of the IAA synthesis."

She speaks eloquently. "When you think about a wound on a plant and the plant is spewing out its insides, bleeding out antimicrobial molecules, there is some evidence they will synthesize at the site and microbes are arrested. But microbes at a distance make tentacles that little by little reach the site of entry. The IAA is recognized by receptors in yeast. A signal turns a DNA switch to hypergrowth."

Wait a minute. I have to ask if I have it right. "So IAA is like a microbial language?"

To my amazement, she confirms this weird science. "Yes," she says. "IAA is a ubiquitous molecule synthesized from the amino acid tryptophan. It's a communication device on a molecular level. A signal," she adds, as if I weren't already impressed, "and it has a distinct smell."

The conversion continues, but really, I am at my absorption level and I begin to scribble down her words automatically, unable to keep up with the ideas. A few times, I have to ask her to repeat herself to be sure. Happily patient with me, she conveys a substantial amount of amazing information in every phrase. I ask her how yeast comes to inhabit the fruit skin in the first place. The answer is something I should have known. After all, we are speaking about a fungus that, like a mushroom, sends countless spores into the air that find their way into every nook and cranny touched by the wind. But Rao, in her kindness, lets me think it was a smart question after all, when she tells me how resilient and truly ubiquitous fungi are. "Spores," she says, "just hang around forever."

After hanging up, I noticed I haven't touched my beer. So I sit back and take a long drink. Clearly I am done working for today, but like Reeta Rao, Andrea Stanley, Bryan Greenhagen, Ben Roesch and Cliff

Hatch, when I am done working, I enjoy thinking about my work. And now I am thinking about a beer I've not yet had with barley grown in the field and hops growing in the yard and yeast that's just been hanging around the orchard. I know I'll find it.

FARMER BREWER

From the beginning of Valley Malt in the autumn of 2010, to the publication of this story in 2015, the locavore beer movement has surged. Five years ago there were four North American craft maltsters, Colorado Malting Company in Alamosa, Colorado, Malterie Frontenac in Montreal, Canada, Michigan Malt in Shepherd, Michigan, and Rebel Malting Company in Reno, Nevada. At this time, by my count, there are thirty-two craft maltsters in fourteen states, plus one in Canada.

Consider this. Even a small malt house represents hundreds of acres of profitable cropland for small, family owned, often organic farms. If they average just half of the annual acreage now under contract to Valley Malt, that would be 125 acres each, which equals more than 4,000 acres of land. In reality, this a very conservative estimate. However, even double that much farmland would be small stuff on the monocultured Midwestern prairie. Yet, most of the farms that supply craft maltsters are located closer to the marketplace, where there is intense economic development pressure—code words for bulldoze and pave.

Take Cascade Maltings, for example. In the midst of a bitter New England winter under threat of a snowstorm, brewers, farmers and prospective maltsters assembled for Valley Malt's 2014 Farmer Brewer Conference at Amherst College. Bill Verbeten of Cornell University spoke about the nutritional requirements of malting barley. Wormtown Brewery's Ben Roesch conducted a seminar on opening a brewery. Nickolas Bokulich, from the University of California Davis, shed light on "microbial terroir." There were several other presentations, and yes, there were some wonderful beers, including a dark sour by Wormtown and a Pinnacle Saison by High Horse Brewing in Amherst in collaboration with The People's Pint. This beer got its name from a variety of barley that Valley Malt recommends for its resistance to fungus.

As we enjoyed the taste of locavore beers, introductions were made and I met Paul Adams. He'd come out from Seattle, Washington, where he is opening a malt house named for the Cascade Mountain range, which bisects that state on a line running north and south.

"We plan to get all of our grain from within 150 miles of Seattle," he said. On his mission to find local grain, he is not alone. To promote grain farming west of the Cascades, Washington State and Oregon State Universities, together with Seattle's Fremont Brewing, sponsored the Cascadia Grains Conference with a mission to bring diverse grain production to the region for use in baking, animal feed and brewing. Like in the Northeast, northwestern grain farmers had once supplied the local markets, but that has been lost.

Among the greatest challenges of farmers in areas like these is the high cost of land. Just like in Massachusetts, the real estate prices in the Seattle area put pressure on open spaces as people commute greater distances in hopes of more affordable living. In 2013, according to Kiplinger Publications, Seattle area real estate prices rose about 20 percent. This can also cause household budgets to tighten, making local and often pricier farm products less affordable. Local farms need customers whose revenue keeps pace with the increasing costs of living. Enter breweries.

Growing nationally at 15 percent, craft brewing is a healthy industry that requires large amounts of agricultural inputs, especially malt. Farmers take notice. In addition, according to the Brewers Association there are 2,700 craft breweries in the US with another 1,500 in planning. As more brewers try to get their brand noticed, incentive to distinguish one beer from another increases. Tapping the existing local food market by supporting small farms can help garner some attention for these start-ups.

Notable brewers as well, such as Dogfish Head, New Belgium, and Brooklyn Brewery have used craft malt. Rogue Ales in Oregon built its own malt house recently. Farmer Brewer legislation that provides a license to brewers using some amount of local ingredients in their beer, has been passed in New York, New Jersey, Virginia and Maryland resulting in dozens of new farm-based businesses in the first year. In New York alone, there are at least twenty-seven brand new breweries, many of them tacked onto an existing farm—a direct result of this new law. Brewers are getting in touch with their agricultural roots. More and more the craft brewing boom is recreating the best of the past as a model for the future.

IF IT CAN HAPPEN HERE . . .

In late 2013, we packed the family into the car for a road trip out to Corning, New York to visit friends from my Portsmouth Brewery days and to listen to the David Grisman Quintet perform. This was a getaway, a family retreat, strictly vacation. I still managed to work a little research into the voyage. A six-hour drive will require at least one stop to eat, right? The sustenance of a little liquid bread—emphasis on little when driving—always helps make the ride more enjoyable.

Some poking around the internet and I found a perfect lunch spot in Albany just under halfway to our destination. The Albany Pump Station provided the eats, but I recall with appreciation beer made by in-house brewery C.H. Evans. The cask conditioned version of their Session IPA received a liberal dose of hops including twenty pounds of wet hops from Indian Ladder Farms in Altamont. A very pale color belied rich flavors of late summer blooms and ripe fruit aromas wiped clean with a sturdy bitterness and malt flavor like crackers. The understated cask carbonation helped mellow a potential for sharp bitterness in this one. Together with my salad I was ready to continue on the road.

As it turns out, the ride was treacherous due to lake effect snow squalls. As Route 88 from Rotterdam to Binghamton and then 86 through Elmira wound us between the stark hillsides and dramatic valleys, the scenery alternated from breathtaking to troubling, as black clouds could be seen approaching under the hilltops and we approached them. With the clouds generally advancing from the northwest and the road following the natural curving path around the steepest parts of the hills, I could see distant farmhouses and barns perched on improbable slopes. Then they would vanish as under an ashen gray cape, the snowy tempest sweeping closer to our little car.

Carefully, we made our way, picking up the pace between columns of blinding snow. Let me say that music, friendship and beer were keenly enjoyed that evening in Corning as the blood came back into my whitened knuckles.

On the way home, again battling legions of snow squalls that galloped over us, we passed through humble Tioga County along the Pennsylvania border. Off exit eight of Route 88, in the town of

Berkshire, population somewhere under 1,500, is Providence Farm. There Natalie and Marty Mattrazzo tend what they call their "non-profit hop farm."

That's how Natalie put it when I spoke to her on the phone. She elaborated by saying with good humor, "We pick everything by hand. After two years, even family members don't answer your calls in August."

They also tried growing malting barley, but, according to Natalie, found that the beer made with it "tasted like dirt." As it turns out, they laugh at this failed farming endeavor, still insisting that, as the name Providence indicates, this farm is a gift from God. After all, Natalie reasoned, there are farmers around who know what they're doing. "We are more than happy to pay good money for our malting barley," she said.

At first getting farmers to grow it at all was a challenge. "Farmers couldn't even remember ancestors who'd grown malting barley," she said. "It's tough to grow because all the disease resistance has been bred out of it." That's because in the western grain belt, summers are dryer than in upstate New York and resistance to disease is not essential. Once again, the spirit of enterprise among farmers made the production of malting barley possible.

While the Mattrazzo's couldn't figure out how to grow the stuff, they know well what to do with it next. In 2013, their FarmHouse Malt sold sixteen tons of malted barley to area brewers and distillers, including Empire Brewing Company out of Syracuse, New York. For the 2014 New York City Beer Week, Empire made a Wheat Wine with Valley Malt wheat and FarmHouse Malt barley.

In 2014, the Mattrazzo's goal was to sell thirty tons of malt contracted from 100 acres of area farmland. They're also running the FarmHouse Brewery alongside the malt house, making—what else?—farmhouse beers with New York terroir. In addition, aspiring maltsters are beating their door down for malting lessons. So, twice a month, Marty puts on a six-hour seminar that has a waiting list of four months. The intense and rapidly increasing interest in making malt from local grain is something the Mattrazzo's cultivate into one third of the malt house income.

Much of what the Mattrazzo's pass on they learned from experience. The lessons are often drawn from mistakes and failures. "Being first doesn't mean we know everything," Natalie pointed out. "My husband always says, 'Pioneers die. Settlers thrive.' You make all the mistakes others learn from. All our mistakes are showcased."

All those blunders and ignorant undertakings have taught them well. "We're making beer and we're making malt, and we're making money," Natalie said. "So, we're not failing anymore, but I have to tell the truth."

As for the Hudson Valley, farms there are flush with this new opportunity as well. Stopping again in Albany, New York on that "vacation," we dashed in to pick up a very special bottle. We didn't have to venture very far from the I-90 exit to find Oliver's Beverage Center, essentially a warehouse of great beer. There I located what I sought—The Divinator. Created by The Beer Diviner of Bly Hollow, this beer is made with 100 percent New York grown Cascade hops. At 11 percent alcohol, it packs a wallop, though not a boozy taste. The ratio of hop flavors to malt flavors was about even, with both aspects lighting up the taste buds. The malt was deep amber, woodsy, almost cognac-like. The hops kept a gingery, lemon zest tingle to match the heavy malt.

I'd had my second New York beer containing local hops. This is a trend that will be more common in coming years as hop farmers now have a dedicated market, thanks to the Farm Brewery legislation passed in Albany. Any brewery using at least 20 percent New York hops, as well as 20 percent of all other local ingredients, is allowed to sell beer at farmers markets and by the glass at up to five of their own off-site locations.

Here's the kicker. This is just the start. Over the coming years, the threshold of local ingredients will be stepped up in two stages until, in 2024, brewers with this license will be required to use 90 percent New York grown ingredients. Just watch how other states follow this model of farm supporting legislation. Grow New York!

STONEMAN, MONKS & MAGIC IN THE PLYMOUTH WOODS

Another huge step forward in the northeastern beer scene is the recent arrival of the one and only Trappist brewery in the United States. Spencer Trappist Ale is the only beer outside of Belgium made by Trappist monks. The Abbey itself isn't new, having been established in Spencer, Massachusetts in 1950 after fires forced several moves. Not only does this enhance New England's portfolio of breweries, but it brings the Trappist sense of agriculture and terroir to the scene with an unbroken link to methods developed by the ancients. This pre-industrial tradition can be seen on the grounds of St. Joseph's Abbey where the Spencer Brewery operates. There, in fields of perennial fruits used to make Trappist Preserves, and acres of pasture for raising livestock for the monastery, barley has been planted. Naturally, plans are in place to have it malted at Valley Malt. Thus, old meets new in a way that supports tradition and contributes to the future security of our farmlands.

Like the Mattrazzo's, these monks give thanks to God for their land and for the fruit of that land, namely beer.

Beer of the land is something Justin Korby understands. His Stoneman Brewery in Colrain, Massachusetts uses 100 percent local malt and hops, including grain he grows himself. He also markets his beer exclusively through the Community Supported Agriculture model of paid shares. Korby embodies the full meaning of farmer brewer. With a beard like a dense overgrowth of vines and little wire rim spectacles in front of eyes that sparkle with constant amusement, Korby seems as jolly as old Saint Nick. Why not? He's now able to combine his love for farming and brewing—something that didn't seem possible only a few short years ago.

Another new brewery owner I met at the Farmer Brewer Conference was Paul Nixon, whose Independent Fermentations Brewing is licensed in Plymouth, Massachusetts. While Nixon uses Valley Malt and local hops, he is not a grower at this time, but he could be called a gatherer brewer. On a foray into the local forest, Nixon came across a patch of wild blueberries. Like Bryan Greenhagen of Mystic Brewing, Nixon picked the berries for their yeast. The batch I got to try was made on an experimental five gallon scale, but the results were so impressive that Nixon plans to try again for commercial production.

I asked him why he thought it might be a good idea to brew with wild yeast. He explained that of the three major influences on a beer's flavor—malt, hops and yeast—yeast is under-appreciated. Among the beers with flavors dominated by microbes is Saison. "I love the barnyard flavors of Saison," Nixon said. "I want to take that and go all sorts of places."

So, he brewed a batch of Saison, then split it up and pitched one half with a commercially cultured Saison yeast. The other, he pitched with yeast from the blueberries. "I was shocked," he said. The Saison yeast produced good results, but the blueberries were outstanding. Again, like with Mystic, Nixon did not use the blueberries themselves in the beer, but only the yeast that inhabited the skin. The yeast provided vibrant flavors of ripe berries and fruit blossom aromatics, yet it finished as dry as an autumn breeze.

The 22-ounce bottle Nixon kindly let me try was gone too soon even though, as the beer dwindled, I took tiny sips to make it last. His recipe calls for Valley Malt's Pils, wheat, and Vienna malts, as well as locally sourced Magnum, Hallertau, Willamette and Sterling hops. When it gets to market this could be the first completely local beer available— Massachusetts-sourced water, malt, hops and yeast. Then it's only a matter of time until everyone knows the northeast beer terrain is well worth savoring.

As I sniffed and sipped and swished this palate pleasing brew, I tried to put words to the flavors. Sometimes it can be pretty difficult to define exactly what a flavor is. That's part of what's so exciting about craft beer. The combination of four ingredients leads to a great many complex blends; molecules are broken down, chemical reactions create new bonds and the living liquid teems with interactions.

Scientists still do not understand how every component in beer contributes to the sensory experience. Throw in an unknown, like a wild yeast . . . new flavors are almost certainly being discovered in defiance of established styles. After all, what matters most is that we enjoy what we imbibe, not whether one beer is like another beer so we can compare and rank. We know what we like when we taste it even if it is like nothing that we've had before. I am definitely pursuing further studies on the subject . . . just to be sure.

HOMEFIELD

I grew up in a baseball household. Five boys, a pair of ball fields behind our house, a father who coached for more than thirty years—I thought of baseball all the time. I loved it. Then came a movie called *Field of Dreams*. I never saw the movie because I thought it would be way too corny. Ahem. In this movie, the idea of baseball and farm fields were linked to a day when distance was farther and time went more slowly. Another movie, *The Natural* left no doubt that farms and baseball were companions in a long ago place—a place where some of those farms grew grain for beer drinkers nearby.

Regardless of nostalgia, I found myself with my brother Matt on a jet to Texas to visit Mike, our oldest brother. Our agenda was beer, food, baseball and music in that order. By now you know me and you know that I looked for Texas-grown beer. Spoiler alert: I found it and it was awesome.

The first words I heard as we walked through the Austin airport were from a fellow with a paunch over his buckle, wearing a white cowboy hat. I was looking for the men's room and he was sitting at a table with a companion drinking coffee. He was apparently telling a story. All I heard was, "I had a beer in one hand and a gun in the other." That's when I knew I wasn't in New England anymore. I had to smile. It's good to get away.

My Texan brother picked up my other Yankee brother and me, and took us immediately to Black's Barbeque in Lockheart, just outside of Austin, where the sign says they're open eight days a week. Our Texan kin schooled us in what to order and I ended up with a slab of fatty brisket that tasted like smoked butter. Fortunately I also had the perfect accompaniment of cole slaw, half-sour pickle, and whole pickled red Jalapeño. Spice and smoke and succulent meat and a Shiner dark lager to wash it down. For dessert, the restaurant, full of baseball-uniformed kids and cowboy boot-wearing moms, broke into a rendition of *Happy Birthday* for the Mr. Black whose black and white images are all over the wall. He's now very white and quite elderly, but he nodded his head in mutual appreciation. As I write this, I am trying to make my own hardwood-smoked brisket on a converted gas grill by chopping chunks off an old hickory log and laying them around the coals every hour or two.

At my request, after our fill of barbecue, we were off to Black Star Co-op Pub & Brewery for a taste of Texas malt. We drove through the typical highway and shopping plaza district and stopped at a number of lights. From the backseat, I passed the minutes looking out the window.

As we idled near a gas station, a man in white tank-top, white shorts and white sneakers, donning white earplug headphones began to perform a familiar dance. He was feinting and deking and dribbling an invisible basketball between his legs as he made his way across the parking lot. Then he performed a graceful lay-up . . . for an imaginary two points. After high-fiving his ghost teammates, he back shuffled down court to play defense.

I tried to get my video phone going, but by then the light turned green and traffic pulled us on. It looked like a good game. At the next light, in front of another gas station, a man juggled bowling pins. I get it; Austin is weird. I was having fun already.

Black Star is located in a mixed-use development that seems to be brand new. Apartment units share a parking lot with a commercial building where the brewery is located. July in central Texas—the sun felt like a chili pepper rubbed on your skin. Inside looked like an ordinary brew pub, but something was completely different than any brew pub I'd ever been to, and as you know, I've been to a few. We stood just inside the door and were blocked by a few people standing in line ahead of us, even though the place was mostly empty.

Being the forward sort and impatiently thirsty, I inquired of the guy in front of me. He explained that we order food and beer at the front of the line. Okay, we stand and wait. In a moment, we order at a register, like in a deli. Except in a deli I order once. A liverwurst sandwich doesn't make me want to order a couple more. Here, when my beer is done, I look and see ten new people have walked in, forming a queue. I have a line to get in, instead of a server to fetch it for me.

Figuring we could get our next beer faster by going somewhere else, it occurred to me that I should pay someone for the first round. So I went to the front of the line and asked the man at the register if I needed to wait in line to pay. He said yes, but made an exception for us and we left with conflicted feelings.

On the one hand the beer was great. On the other hand, I wish it were easier to get a second one. When I tried to tip, I was told they do not except tips because they are paid a living wage. I bet a waitress would do even better.

My reluctance to submit to the line may have been from having already gone twice through airport security that day. Really, Black Star is pretty damn cool. Where else but a brewpub, where both the restaurant and the brewing industry have been most creative, would you expect things to be, well, different? For instance, the Co-op part of the name references the ownership model.

As a cooperative, there is no single person who is an owner. Black Star is owned by more than 3,000 customers, workers and organizations. Decisions are made democratically and the employees are paid a livable wage, meaning if they work forty hours, they won't need welfare. It's a calculation based on the cost of living, so the actual rate changes year to year and place to place. This model is the opposite of large retail corporations that pay minimum wage, a rate that leads to serious poverty and welfare enrollment in this country. It didn't sit right with me that my tip was rejected, however. I wanted to show appreciation and, having come from afar to visit this particular place, I cannot be a regular supporter. If I lived in Austin, however, I sure would find time to stop by because what matters the most was very good indeed.

If I could have only one, I chose well, though my brothers also had excellent beer. Mine was Hubris. A pale ale made with Blacklands wheat and barley malt, as well as Sorachi Ace hops to give it a pinch of lemon on a fresh malt palette. The folks at this brew pub are stoked to be able to get malt nearby.

According to their website, "When we use our preferred pale malt from Weyermann, the malt travels from Bamberg, Germany. We really like Weyermann Malts, and they taste delicious. However, we have concerns about generating a high carbon footprint from shipping overseas as well as the possibility of not getting the freshest malt possible. There are maltsters in North America, but you have the same issues, just a little less of a footprint. Now imagine being able to get the majority of the weight of your ingredients from Leander! Not only that, once we're done with the grain, it is donated to a local rancher in East Austin for cow feed. That is a great local cycle of sustainability."

More than that, they point to proof that Blacklands malt is better where it matters most—the flavor. Again, from the website, "In a blind tasting performed by our three brewers, we compared Weyermann pale malt and Blacklands pale malt. All three of us chose the Blacklands malt for its fresh aroma and taste. And finally, the true test, while brewing our batch of Hubris with the Pale Moon malt, we had a wonderful efficiency and brewhouse performance."

Here's the dose of salt. The Pale Moon barley malt used in this beer is malted in Leander by Blacklands owner, Brandon Ade, but it is grown in Colorado.

"We just harvested our first Texas barley," Ade said in July 2014. Up until then the only malting grain grown in Texas had been wheat, meaning there's Texas-grown wheat malt in Hubris and Colorado-grown barley malted in Texas.

Granted, compared with Riverbend Malt House in Asheville, North Carolina and Valley Malt in Hadley, Massachusetts, the current impact of Blacklands Malt is tiny. But consider this: in his first growing season, Ade set his sights high. "We were shooting for 120 acres last fall," he said. "Only half got in the ground, thanks to Mother Nature. This fall it was too wet to plant. Ironic, considering you hear a lot about the drought."

Ade refers to the ongoing drier than normal conditions across Texas and the anomaly that was October 2013. Average October rainfall in Austin is 3.88 inches. Unlike the Northeast, where both winter and summer grain are grown, Texas farmers have only one season, given the daily high temperatures over 100 degrees in the summer. Planting time is October in the Blacklands, but that year, more than 13 inches of rain fell, washing away much of the seed.

Next year is always bound to be better and Ade has his sights set on a lot more Texas grown malting grains. "Next time," he said, "the goal is 160 acres at one ton per acre." That could make over one hundred thousand gallons of Texas-grown beer.

And why not? After all, the Blacklands that give Ade's malt house its name are a unique ecosystem, and African like savanna. These grasslands run north and south in roughly the shape of hip-high boots. An endangered southern prairie, it got its name from the rich dark soil, the result of frequent, widespread fires. The historical foraging of bison, and now cattle, keeps forest growth at bay.

One reason Blacklands has been able to go from zero to 160 acres in such a short time is thanks to the help of Texas A&M University recommending barley varieties that could succeed in the unique Texas grassland climate. Field trials are ongoing. Here, as in most other places where farmers are trying to grow for brewers, the local agricultural colleges have stepped in to offer assistance.

This new venture is here now, primarily because of the will-power of Brandon Ade. Within three months of first considering what it would be like to malt barley, Blacklands was born. Less than two years later the Austin beer scene, one that offers an array of outstanding breweries, had been changed for the better.

That's saying something for a computer engineer who took a three-week primer course in malting at a technical school in Winnipeg, Canada. Ade said the class was useful, but "I learned the most from studying equipment design. I learned a lot through that process and reading everything I could get on the subject."

With a background as a computer engineer, Ade has the aptitude for digging into technical information and organizing processes, which was essential in the quick launch of the malt house. But computer engineering is desk work, and Ade wanted to do more. "I was missing the connection with making something with my hands," he said. "This is my livelihood now. I work more than I do anything else. Being connected to agriculture and the brewing culture is really satisfying."

That brewing culture has welcomed Ade's malt with open excitement. When I was there, three top-notch breweries offered up beer made with Blacklands malt. Aside from Black Star Co-op, Pinthouse Pizza has a SMaSH on tap, a single malt and single hop pale ale using the Pale Moon American two-row malt.

Other breweries in town that have been buying from Blacklands include Kamala, Hops & Grain and Twisted X. The most revered brewery in Texas, and perhaps all of the southern United States—Jester King—also loves Blacklands malt.

Jester King has already tried to emphasize the terrain in their beer-making. They have become renowned, in part, because of their use of wild yeast harvested from the wind and the landscape. According to their website, "Adding barley and wheat grown and malted in central Texas to our beer making equation is something we're excited about."

When I was there, Jester King featured Blacklands in their Le Petit Prince Farmhouse Table Beer, a low alcohol brew for session style enjoyment.

Home Sweet Home

You know we have made progress as a culture and, hopefully, as a species, when beer can be completely local and spread coast to coast at the same time.

Consistency is important to a brewery's success in most cases. From my keyboard there is no argument with that, but there is a counterpoint. There is a way to brand inconsistency. What the local fields offer is one-of-a-kind beers. As Wormtown breaks ground with their new production facility that has many, myself especially, whetting their thirsts, and so many other wannabe-Wormtowns chase that model down the road, one beer is walking its own path. We call it Homefield.

I'll have to start at the beginning. In writing this book, I've found myself in a great many conversations. At my son's ball games, for example, other parents make small talk and ask, "So what are you up to?" Word gets around. That guy is writing a book about beer. Must be grueling research, they jest. I have been peppered with questions. Have any good IPA's lately? Have you been to that brewery up in Vermont? Most often, I get this question: "When are you going to make some of this local beer?"

Believe me, I cannot take a hint. I am dull, dense and, frankly, too self-centered to get it when someone is handing me a great idea. I had to be asked several times before I started asking myself. Why don't I brew a beer made with all local ingredients and offer it up? Why don't I just do that? One reason—I don't own a commercial brewery.

After months of research and consideration, countless consultations on the front porch with my collaborator, a couple meetings with the good folks at Rapscallion Brewery in Sturbridge, Homefield is being made. Using 100 percent Valley Malt and 100 percent local hops in collaboration with Suzanne and me, brewer Shaun Radzuik will be making 300 gallons of a hoppy session ale in nine different batches over the coming year. Each batch will vary with the variety of the ingredients and the timing of the beer.

As for the response, well, you remember the movie. Build it and they will come.

Resources
Where to find grain, malt, hops, locavore beer, and more

This is not an attempt at a complete list, which is impossible considering many beers made with local ingredients are one-time-only brews. Instead, this is meant to be used as a starting point for locavores.

Connecticut

Hops

Bodhichitta Farms, Prospect
(203) 244-4340

Driscoll Hop Yard, Stratford
On Twitter: @cthopguy

Farming 101, Newtown
(203) 917-9979, www.101brushyhill.com

Roseledge Country Inn and Farm Shoppe, Preston
(860) 892-4739, www.roseledge.com

Wellstone Farm, Higganum
(860) 345-3183, wellstonefarm@gmail.com

Grains

Still River Farm, Coventry
(860) 742-5717

Locavore Brewers

Cambridge House Brew Pub, Granby
Uses Valley Malt in many brews.
(860) 653-2739, www.cbhgranby.com

Thomas Hooker Brewing Company, Bloomfield
Uses estate grown hops in their season.
(860) 242-4447, www.hookerbeer.com

Willimantic Brewing Company, Willimantic
Uses hops from Winding Brook Sugar House and unmalted cracked wheat from Great River Farm.
(860) 423-6777, www.willibrew.com

AINE

HOPS

Aroostook Hops, Westfield
(207) 429-8105, www.aroostookhops.com

Elm Hill Farm, Monroe
(207) 338-0419

Irish Hill Hops, Monroe
(207) 338-2637

Prime Hops of Maine, Benton
www.facebook.com/PrimeHopsOfMaine

Rock Island Hop Farm, Springvale
www.rockislandhopfarm.com

The Hop Yard, Fort Fairfield/Gorham
www.thehopyard.com

GRAINS

Grange Corner Farm, Lincolnville
(207) 706-6912, www.facebook.com/grangecornerfarm

Heritage Wheat Conservancy, Waterville
www.growseed.org

Lake Shore Farm, St. David
(207) 728-4566

Qualey Farms Inc., Benedicta
(207) 365-4385

LOCAVORE BREWERS

Allagash Brewing Company, Portland
Uses Valley Malt pilsner in their annual Hugh Malone Belgian IPA; uses native yeast in traditional fermentation processes.
(207) 878-5385, www.allagash.com

Bunker Brewing Company, Portland
Uses hops from Rock Island Hop Farm.
(207) 450-5014, www.bunkerbrewingco.com

Maine Beer Company, Freeport
Uses Valley Malt in their Collaboration Time series.
(207) 221-5711, www.mainebeercompany.com

Oxbow Beer, Newcastle
Occasionally uses Valley Malt in their Freestyle series.
(207) 315-5962, www.oxbowbeer.com

Peak Organic Brewing Company, Portland
Uses Valley Malt in most beers, including their Local Series of brews with ingredients from a single state; Valley Malt BSA member.
(207) 586-5586, www.peakbrewing.com

Rising Tide Brewing Company, Portland
Uses Valley Malt rye in their Daybreak Pale Ale.
(207) 370-2337, www.risingtidebrewing.com

Sebago Brewing, Portland
Uses Maine grown hops in their annual Local Harvest Ale.
www.sebagobrewing.com

MASSACHUSETTS

MALT

Valley Malt, Hadley
(413) 349-9098, www.valleymalt.com

HOPS

Cedar Spring Herb Farm, Harwich
(508) 430-4372, www.cedarspringherbfarm.com

Clover Hill Farm, Hardwick
Used by Wormtown Brewery; homebrewer pick your own.
(978) 257-2390, cranaussie@aol.com

Divoll's Farm, Royalston
(978) 602-5583

Dover Farm, Dover
(617) 784-4123, www.doverfarmcsa.com

Four Star Farms, Northfield
(413) 498-2968, www.fourstarfarms.com

Gateways Farm, Weston
Used by Watch City Brewing.
(781) 237-6576

Goldthread Organic Herb Farm & Apothecary, Conway
(413) 625-8167, www.goldthreadapothecary.com

Great Cape Herbs, Brewster
(508) 896-5900, www.greatcape.com

Hancock Shaker Village, Pittsfield
(413) 443-0188, www.hancockshakervillage.org

Langwater Farm, North Easton
(508) 205-9665, www.langwaterfarm.com

Little Pamet Farm, Truro
(508) 349-7965, www.littlepametfarm.com

Marini Farm, Ipswich
Used by Ipswich Ale Brewery.
(978) 356-0430, www.marinifarm.com

Grains

Czajkowski Farm, Hadley
(413) 237-2615, www.czajkowskifarm.com

Four Star Farms, Northfield
(413) 498-2968, www.fourstarfarms.com

Misty Brook Farm, Barre
(413) 477-8234, mistybrookorganicfarm@yahoo.com

Pastor Blacksmith Farm, Concord
(978) 451-4566, info@pastorblacksmithfarm.com

Pioneer Valley Heritage Grain, Amherst
www.localgrain.org

Slow Tractor Farm, Hadley
Owned by Valley Malt.
valleymalt.com/slow-tractor-farm

Upinngil Farm, Gill
(413) 863-4431, www.upinngil.com

LOCALLY GROWN HOMEBREW INGREDIENTS

DIY Brewing Supply, Ludlow
(413) 547-1110

Modern Homebrew Emporium, Cambridge
(617) 498-0400, www.beerbrew.com

LOCAVORE BREWERS

Abandoned Building Brewery, Easthampton
Uses Valley Malt and the brewery's own hops.
(413) 282-7062, www. abandonedbuildingbrewery.com

Barrington Brewery & Restaurant, Great Barrington
Uses fresh harvest local hops in September and October.
(413) 528-8282, www. barringtonbrewery.net

Blatant Brewery, Williamsburg
Uses local malt in anniversary ales.
www.blatantbrewery.com

Brewmaster Jack, contract brewer at Paper City Brewery, Holyoke
Uses at least 25 percent Valley Malt in every batch.
(413) 367-7190, www.brewmasterjack.com

Buzzards Bay Brewing, Westport
Grows some of their own hops.
(508) 636-2288, www. buzzardsbrew.com

Cambridge Brewing Company, Cambridge
Uses Valley Malt in numerous batches, including the Valley Girl series and the annual Spring Training. Also uses Four Star hops in many batches, including several annual 100 percent locally grown releases.
(617) 494-1994, www.cambridgebrewingcompany.com

Cape Ann Brewing Company, Gloucester
Honey Pilsner includes hops from Thacher's Island; Home Port Pale Ale uses hops from the brewery's fields.
(978) 282-7399, www.capeannbrewing.com

Cisco Brewers, Nantucket
Uses hops from their own farm.
(508) 325-5929, www.ciscobrewers.com

Element Brewing Company, Millers Falls
Uses Valley Malt for annual Spring Intervale release.
(413) 835-6340, www.elementbeer.com

Gardner Ale House, Gardner
Face Off Double IPA uses hops grown by customer.
(978) 669-0122, www. gardnerale.com

Goodfelllow's Brewing Company, Lakeville
Uses hops and other ingredients from Frugal Endeavors Farm.
(774) 766-2691, www. goodfellowsbrewing.com

High Horse Brewing, Amherst
Uses Valley Malt in almost every batch.
(413) 230-3034, www.highhorsebrewing.com

Independent Fermentations, Plymouth
Uses Valley Malt & Four Star Farms in every batch; some indigenous yeast.
(508) 789-9940, www.independentfermentations.com

Ipswich Ale Brewery, Ipswich
Uses Valley Malt and Marini Farms hops for their 5 Mile Ale series, harvests their own Exeter County grain.
(978) 356-3329, www.ipswichalebrewery.com

Jack's Abby Brewing, Framingham
Uses local grain in every batch, uses their own hops and Valley Malt for the Mom & Pop's series.
(508) 872-0900, www.jacksabbybrewing.com

KBC Brewery & Beer Garden, Webster
Uses hops from Four Star Farms in their Blond and IPL.
(508) 671-7711, www. kbcbrewing.com

Mystic Brewery, Chelsea
Native yeast hunter, uses Valley Malt for Old Powderhouse, a wheat wine.
(617) 466-2079, www.mystic-brewery.com

Nashoba Valley Winery, Bolton
Uses Valley Malt in all their beers, as well as estate grown hops.
(978) 779-5521, www.nashobawinery.com

Night Shift Brewing, Everett
Uses Valley Malt rye in the Viva Habanera, and Valley Malt pilsner in the Snow, a "white stout."
(617) 294-4233, www.nightshiftbrewing.com

Northampton Brewery, Northampton
Makes an annual Four Star Harvest Ale and a Four Star Harvest IPA with hops from Four Star Farms in Northfield.
(413) 584-9903, www.northamptonbrewery.com

Notch Brewing Company, *an independent brewer making beer at Ipswich Ale Brewery in Ipswich, Two Roads Brewing Company in Stratford, Connecticut and Kennebunkport Brewing Company in Maine.*
(978) 238-9060, www.notchbrewing.com

Offshore Ale Company, Oak Bluffs
Uses their own hops in Hopps Farm Road Pale Ale.
(508) 693-2626, www.offshoreale.com

Rapscallion Brewery, Sturbridge
Brewers of Homefield; uses hops from Four Star Farms in its Black IPA.
(617) 869-5702, www.drinkrapscallion.com

Stoneman Brewery, Colrain
Making beer with almost 100% local malt and hops, exclusively marketed through a Community Supported Agriculture share program.
(413) 624-5195, www.growbeer.com

The People's Pint, Greenfield
Uses Valley Malt in every batch; often releases 100% local malt/hops beers.
(413) 773-0333, www.thepeoplespint.com

Treehouse Brewing Company, Monson
Occasionally uses hops grown by a customer.
(413) 949-1891, www.treehousebrew.com

Trillium Brewing, Boston
Uses heirloom gains from Valley Malt in many beers including a Danko rye in their Pocket Pigeon Blonde Ale.
(617) 453-8745, www.trilliumbrewing.com

Wachusett Brewing Company, Westminster
Makes an annual limited release Homegrown Hop Ale with hops from the brewer's garden.
(978) 874-9965, www.wachusettbrew.com

Wormtown Brewery, Worcester
"A little Mass in every glass." Uses Valley Malt in every batch, and keeps the MassWhole series going year round using 100 percent local malt and hops.
(774) 239-1555, www.wormtownbrewery.com

NEW HAMPSHIRE

HOPS

Animal House Brewing, Hollis
Homebrewer using hops from his own farm.
www.animalhousebrewing.com

Isinglass River Hops Exchange, Strafford
Growing hops for 7th Settlement Brewing and setting up a hop processing and distribution network.
(603) 664-3880, www.facebook.com/isinglassriverhops

Misty Mountain Farm, Effingham
(603) 539-2210, www.facebook.com/mistymountainfarm

GRAINS

Brookfield Farm, Walpole
(603) 445-5104

Brookford Farm, Canterbury
Grows grain for Throwback Brewery.
(603) 742-4084, www.brookfordfarm.com

Locavore Brewers

7th Settlement Brewery, Dover
Uses local grain in their 1896 Cochecho Winter Wheat.
(603) 373-1001, www.7thsettlement.com

Berts Better Beers, Hooksett
Grows some of their own hops.
(603) 413-5992, www.bertsbetterbeers.com

Earth Eagle Brewing, Portsmouth
Uses local grain and hops.
(603) 817-2773, www.eartheaglebrewings.com

Elm City Brewing Company, Keene
Occasionally uses local wild hops.
(603) 355-3335, www.elmcitybrewing.com

Redhook Brewery, Portsmouth
Backyard Series features Warthog wheat malt from Valley Malt and the brewery's own hops.
www.redhook.com

Smuttynose Brewing Company, Portsmouth
Uses Valley Malt in their Short batch series; Valley Malt BSA member.
(603) 436-4026, www.smuttynose.com

Throwback Brewery, North Hampton
Uses 70 percent local ingredients in everything they make, including local grain, Valley Malt, and local hops; Valley Malt BSA member.
(603) 379-2317, www.throwbackbrewery.com

The Prodigal Brewery, Effingham
Uses hops from their own Misty Mountain Farm.
(603) 539-2210, www.theprodigalbrewery.com

White Birch Brewing, Hooksett
Harvest Ale uses hops grown at Berts Better Beers.
www.whitebirchbrewing.com

Locavore Homebrew Supplies

Kettle to Keg, Suncook
(603) 485-2054, www.kettletokeg.com

NEW YORK

MALT

East Coast Malts, Freeville
Produces base malt; some specialty malts.
(607) 280-1047, www.eastcoastmalts.com

Farmhouse Malt, Newark Valley
Producing 2-row and 6-row base malts for home and commercial brewers.
(607)-227-0638, www.farmhousemalt.com

Flower City Malt Lab, Rochester
(585) 747-4102, www.flowercitymaltlab.com

Henneberg Brewing Company, New Woodstock
(315) 350-4242, www.hennebergbrewing.com

Niagara Malt, Cambria
Grows barley and hops; began malting in 2014.
(716) 861-9887, www.niagaramalt.com

New York Craft Malt, Batavia
Grain farmer began malting in 2014.
(585) 813-5389, www.newyorkcraftmalt.com

Towpath Malt, Canastota
Corey Mosher, mosher.corey@gmail.com

GRAIN

Dream Weaver Farms, Richfield Springs
Gino Labruzzo, (315) 360-0454

J. Glebocki Farms, Goshen
(845) 651-8088, www.glebockifarms.com

Lakeview Organic Grain, Penn Yan
(315) 531-1038, www.lakevieworganicgrain.com

Oechsner Farms, Newfield
Thor Oechsner, (607) 564-7701

Pedersen Farms, Seneca Castle
(315) 781-0482, www.pedersenfarms.com

Hops

Arrowood Farms, Accord
(828) 308-1634, www.arrowoodfarms.com

BitterWind Hop Farm, Trumansburg
(503) 318-2831, www.bitterwindfarm.com

Bluebell Hopyard, Farmington
www.bluebellhopyard.com

Bundschuh's Greenhouses, Macedon
(315) 986-8872, www.bundschuhsgreenhouses.com

Clark Hollow Hops, Fabius
www.clarkhollowhops.com

Dutch Barn Farm, Ft. Plain
(518) 993-4983, www.dutchbarnfarm.com

East Prairie Hop Company, Collins
(716) 867-8735, www.eastprairiefarms.com

Elderbery Herb Farm, Sharon Springs
(518) 284-3727, www.elderberryherbfarm.com

Fiddlehead Creek, Hartford
(518) 632-5505, www.fiddleheadcreek.com

Foothill Hops Bitter End Brewing Company, Munnsville
(315) 495-2451, www.foothillhops.com

Hartwood Farm, Fenner
(315) 655-5652, www.hartwoodfarm.com

High Bines Hop Yard, Ransonville
www.highbines.com

Hip Hops Farm, Brookfield
(315) 857-1185, www.hiphopsfarm.com

HopRidge Farms, Johnsville
www.hopridgefarms.com

Hudson Valley Hoppery, Elizaville
www.hudsonvalleyhoppery.com

McCollum Orchards, Lockport
(716) 730-0703, www.oldfarmnewlife.com

Pedersen Farms, Seneca Castle
(315) 781-0482, www.pedersenfarms.com

Providence Farm, Berkshire
Marty and Natalie Mattrazzo, (607) 227-0638

Riverview Hop Farm, Afton
(607) 648-5931, www.riverviewhopfarm.com

Saratoga Hops, Ballston Spa
518-885-5609, www.saratogahops.com

The Bineyard, Cazenovia
(617) 515-1011, www.thebineyard.com

Valley View Hops, Otisco
Rob McLusky, (315) 439-1445

Whipple Brothers Farms, Kendall
(585) 350-9707, www.whipplebrothersfarms.com

LOCALLY GROWN HOMEBREW INGREDIENTS

Brooklyn Homebrew, Brooklyn
(718) 832-2739, www.brooklyn-homebrew.com

FARMER BREWERS

By law these brewers must use 20 percent New York hops and of the remaining ingredients, 20 percent must be grown in New York. By 2024 the requirements will be for these brewers to use 90 percent New York state ingredients.

Abandon Brewing Company, Penn Yann
Farmhouse brewery; uses locally grown malt and hops.
(585) 209-3276, www.abandonbrewing.com

Adirondack Toboggan Company Microbrewery, Gouverneur
(315) 771-6313, www.adktoboggan.net

BarkEater Craft Brewery, Lowville
(315) 376-2337, www.barkeaterbrewing.com

Barrier Brewing Company, Oceanside
www.barrierbrewing.com

Bly Hollow Brewery and The Beer Diviner, Cherry Plain
Uses Valley Malt and in the Divinator Double IPA, uses all local Cascade hops. Offers CSB memberships; Valley Malt BSA member.
(518) 210-6196, www.thebeerdiviner.com

Brown's Brewing Company, Troy
(518) 273-2337, www.brownsbrewing.com

Climbing Bines Hop Farm, Seneca Lake
(607) 745-0221, www.climbingbineshopfarm.com

Cortland Beer Company, Corltand
(607) 662-4389, www.cortlandbeer.com

Erie Canal Brewing Company, Canastota
Uses 100% local ingredients.
(315) 510-5001, www.eriecanalbrewingcompany.com

Fairport Brewing Company, Fairport
Uses FarmHouse Malt.
(585) 678-6728, www.fairportbrewing.com

FarmHouse Brewery, Newark Valley
Uses their own malt and hops.
(607) 227-0638, www.thefarmhousebrewery.com

Fingerlakes Beer Company, Hammondsport
Uses FarmHouse Malt.
(607) 569-3311, www.fingerlakesbeercompany.com

Good Nature Farm Brewery & Tap Room, Hamilton
Uses Valley Malt in The Nor Easter; uses FarmHouse Malt.
(315) 824-2337, www.goodnaturebrewing.com

Greenport Harbor Brewing Company, Greenport and Peconic
www.greenportharborbrewing.com

Griffin Hill Farm Brewery, Onondaga
www.griffinhillny.com

Gun Hill Brewing Company, Bronx
(718) 881-0010, www.gunhillbrewing.com

Hamburg Brewing Company, Hamburg
www.hamburgbrewing.com

Honey Hollow Brewery, Earlton
www.honeyhollowbrewery.com

Hopshire Farm & Brewery, Freeville
Growing hops, using NY hops and other local ingredients in every batch.
(607) 279-1243, www.hopshire.com

Indian Ladder Farmstead Brewery & Cidery, Altamont
Grows their own hops.
(518) 765-2956, www.indianladderfarmsteadbrewery.com

Long Ireland Beer Company, Riverhead
(631) 403-4303, www.longirelandbrewing.com

Moustache Brewing Company, Riverhead
Uses FarmHouse Malt.
(631) 591-3250, www.moustachebrewing.com

Other Half Brewing, Brooklyn
(347) 987-3527, www.otherhalfbrewing.com

Plan Bee Farm Brewery, Fishkill
www.planbeefarmbrewery.com

Rooster Fish Brewing, Watkins Glen
(607) 535-9797, www.roosterfishbrewing.com

The North Brewery, Endicott
Uses FarmHouse Malt.
(607) 785-0524, www.northbrewery.com

The VB Brewery, Victor
(585) 902-8166, www.thevbbrewery.com

Twisted Rail Brewing Company, Canandaigua
(585) 797-7437, www.twistedrailbrewing.com

Yard Owl Craft Brewery, New Platz
www.yardowlcraftbrewery.com

Locavore Brewers

Argyle Brewing Company, Greenwich
(518) 692-2585, www.argylebrewing.com

Birdland Brewing Company, Horseheads
Uses local hops and grain in Osprey Ale, uses Farmhouse Malt.
(607) 769-2337, www.birdlandbrewingco.com

Brooklyn Brewery, Brooklyn
Uses Valley Malt's New York grown grain for NY Grown series, as well as New York hops; used 500 pounds of upstate winter wheat for Brooklyn High Line Elevated Wheat; Valley Malt BSA member.
www.brooklynbrewery.com

Empire Brewing Company, Syracuse
Made a wheat wine for New York City's 2014 Beer Week using red winter wheat from Valley Malt, 2-row barley from FarmHouse Malt and Cascade hops from New York State; also brews in Brooklyn.
(315) 475-2337, www.empirebrew.com

Fire Island Beer Co., Ocean Beach
Pumpkin Barrel Ale includes hops from Pompey Mountain Hops Farm.
(631) 482-3118, www.fireislandbeer.com

Galaxy Brewing Company, Binghamton
Grows hops and uses hops from local farms in their Galaxy NY Harvest Ale.
(607) 217-7074, www.galaxybrewingco.com

Green Wolf Brewing Company, Middleburgh
Uses FarmHouse Malt; sells CSA memberships.
(518) 872-2503, www.greenwolfales.com

Ithaca Beer Company, Ithaca
Uses FarmHouse Malt.
(607) 273-0766, www.ithacabeer.com

Keegan Ales, Kingston
Uses hops from their own fields.
(845) 331-2739, www.keeganales.com

KelSo Beer Company, Brooklyn
Look for the Rauchbier made with Valley Malt cherrywood smoked triticale; locavore beer series KelSo edible ale.
www.kelsobeer.com

Rare Form Brewing Company, Troy
Uses FarmHouse Malt.
(518) 326-4303, www.rareformbrewing.com

Red Hawk Brewing, Syracuse
Uses FarmHouse Malt.
www.redhawkbrewing.com

Saranac Brewery, Utica
Uses FarmHouse Malt in their all NY State brews.
www.saranac.com

Sixpoint Brewery, Brooklyn
Uses wild yeast collected from brewery's rooftop.
(917) 696-0438, www.sixpoint.com

Water Street Brewing Company, Binghamton
Uses FarmHouse Malt.
(607) 217-4546, www.waterstreetbrewingco.com

RHODE ISLAND

HOPS

Fellow Workers Farm, Providence
(845) 514-3519, www.fellowworkersfarm.com

New Urban Farmers, Pawtucket
www.newurbanfarmers.com

Ocean State Hops, Exeter
www.oceanstatehops.com

LOCAVORE BREWERS

Newport Storm Brewery, Newport
Occasionally uses Valley Malt; uses Chinook hops from Ocean State Hops in their India Point Ale.
(401) 849-5232, www.newportstorm.com

Tilted Barn Brewery, Exeter
Started by Ocean State Hops.
www.facebook.com/tiltedbarnbrewery

Locavore Homebrew Supplies

Craft Brews Supplies, Wyoming
(401) 539-2337, www.craftbrewssupplies.com

Vermont

Grains

Butterworks Farm, Westfield
www.butterworksfarm.com

Morningstar Meadow Farm, Glover
(802) 525-4672

Tio Grain Farm, Shoreham
(802) 948-2423

Hops

Addison Hop Farm, Addison
(802) 989-4214, www.addisonhopfarm.com

Square Nail Hops Farm, Ferrisburgh
(802) 355-3309
www.facebook.com/pages/Square-Nail-Hops-Farm/108388169211853

Locavore Brewers

Vermont Pub & Brewery, Burlington
Brews a series called All Vermont Grains and Hops Project.
(802) 865-0500, www.vermontbrewery.com

Bobcat Cafe & Brewery, Bristol
Uses local hops in most of their small batches and grows some of their own.
(802) 453-3311

Malthouses Across the US

California Malting Company, Santa Barbara, California
www.californiamaltingco.com

Eckert Malting & Brewing, Chico, California
www.eckertmaltingandbrewing.com

Colorado Malting Company, Alamosa, Colorado
www.coloradomaltingcompany.com
Used by New Belgium Brewing, Sierra Nevada, Oskar Blues, Ska Brewing, Wynkoop Brewing, Goose Island, Flying Dog, Dogfish Head, Rocky Mountain Brewery, Sun King, Black Shirt, Caution: Brewing Co., Dad & Dudes Breweria, Our Mutual Friend, San Luis Valley Brewing, Three Barrel, Scotzin & Bros., Glenwood Canyon Brewpub, Wiley Roots Brewing, Dostal Alley, Shamrock Brewing, AC Golden, Gunnison, Taos Mesa Brewing, Cumbre, Powell Street, and Westminster Brewing Company.

Grouse Malting and Roasting Co., Wellington, Colorado
www.grouseco.com
Used by Three Spires Brewing, Tap and Handle, Element Brewing, Aurochs Brewing, Ghostfish Brewing.

Abbott's Mill House, Milford, Delaware
Used by Dogfish Head.

Mammoth Malt, Thawville, Illinois
Used by Moody Tongue Brewing.

Corsair Distillery, Bowling Green, Kentucky
www.corsairartisan.com

Blue Ox Malthouse, Belfast, Maine
www.blueoxmalthouse.com

Amber Fields Malting & Brewing, Frederick, Maryland
www.amberfieldsmb.com
Uses their own malt

Valley Malt, Hadley, Massachusetts
www.valleymalt.com

Great State Malting, Detroit, Michigan
www.greatstatemalting.com

Pilot Malt House, Jenison, Michigan
www.pilotmalthouse.com
Used by EB Coffee and Pub, Gonzo's BiggDogg, Chelsea Alehouse, Four Fathers Brewing, Hop Lot, Northport Brewing, Osgood Brewing, Shorts Brewing, Tibbs Brewing, Tripel Root, Unruly Brewing, and Pigeon Hill. Also available at Northern Brewer Homebrew Supply.

Michigan Malt, Shepherd, Michigan
www.michiganmalt.com
Used by Woodward Ave Brewery, New Holland, Rockford Brewing, Saugatuck Brewing.

Rebel Malting Company, Reno, Nevada
www.rebelmalting.com
Used by Great Basin Brewing Company

New York Craft Malt, Batavia, New York
www.newyorkcraftmalt.com

Niagara Malt, Cambria Center, New York
www.niagaramalt.com/

Riverbend Malt House, Asheville, North Carolina
www.riverbendmalt.com
Used by Hi-Wire Brewing, Burial Beer, Great Raft Beer, Sierra Nevada, Haw River Farmhouse Ales, New Belgium, Wicked Weed, Fonta Flora, Fullsteam Brewing

Rogue Ales & Spirits, Newport, Oregon
www.rogue.com

Gold Rush Malt, Baker City, Oregon
www.goldrushmalt.com

Deer Creek Malthouse, Chester County, Pennsylvania
www.deercreekmalt.com

Keystone Malt, Philadelphia, Pennsylvania
www.keystonemalt.com

Blacklands Malt, Leander, Texas
www.blacklandsmalt.com
Used by Kamala Brewing, Twisted X, Jester King, Hops & Grain, Pinthouse Pizza, and Black Star Co-op.

Peterson Quality Malt, Monkton, Vermont

Skagit Valley Malting Company, Burlington, Washington
www.skagitvalleymalting.com

Cascade Maltings, Seattle, Washington
www.cascademaltings.com

MISCELLANEOUS RESOURCES AND WEB SITES

All About Beer Magazine
www.allaboutbeer.com

American Craft Beer
Best Craft Beers, Breweries, Places Serving Craft Beer
www.americancraftbeer.com

Annual Hops Conference, Vermont
www.uvm.edu/search_results?q_as=Hops%20Conference

Beer Advocate Magazine
www.beeradvocate.com

Beer Festivals Calendar
www.beerfestivals.org

Brewers Association
A Passionate Voice for Craft Brewers
www.brewersassociation.org

Craft Beer
Celebrating the Best of American Beer
www.craftbeer.com

Craft Beer Club *(Beer of the Month Club)*
www.craftbeerclub.com

Craft Brew Alliance
www.craftbrew.com

Craft Maltster's Guild
A community for craft malt
www.craftmalting.com

Cornell University Cooperative Extension
Research on growing malting barley in New York
www.nwnyteam.org/topic.php?id=3

Drink Craft Beer
www.drinkcraftbeer.com

Great American Beer Festival
www.greatamericanbeerfestival.com

Great Brewers
www.greatbrewers.com

The Homebrew Academy
www.homebrewacademy.com

Homebrewers Outpost
www.homebrewers.com

Hops Direct/Puterbaugh Farms
www.hopsdirect.com

Madison County Hop Fest, Oneida, NY
www.mchs1900.org

Northeast Hop Alliance
Growing the hops industry in the Northeast
www.northeasthopalliance.org

Northern Brewer Homebrew Supply
www.northernbrewer.com

Northern Grain Growers Association
www.northerngraingrowers.org

Vermont Hops Project
To increase hop production in Vermont, trial hopyard
www.uvm.edu/extension/cropsoil/hops

About the Author

Jonathan Cook has been brewing beer with homegrown ingredients since 1999, when he and his wife, Suzanne LePage, toured New England brewpubs on their honeymoon. Cook runs the chef's garden at the historic Salem Cross Inn in West Brookfield, Massachusetts and also operates One Acre Farm, raising chickens, hops, and berries.

beerterrain.blogspot.com
www.facebook.com/jonathan.cook.9041